6/00

INTO THE PORCUPINE CAVE

AND OTHER ODYSSEYS

Adventures of an Occasional Naturalist

Also by William W. Warner

~

BEAUTIFUL SWIMMERS: WATERMEN, CRABS,
AND THE CHESAPEAKE BAY

DISTANT WATER: THE FATE OF
THE NORTH ATLANTIC FISHERMAN

AT PEACE WITH ALL THEIR NEIGHBORS: CATHOLICS AND
CATHOLICISM IN THE NATIONAL CAPITAL, 1787-1860

INTO THE PORCUPINE CAVE

AND OTHER ODYSSEYS

Adventures of an Occasional Naturalist

WILLIAM W. WARNER

NATIONAL GEOGRAPHIC

WASHINGTON D.C.

Published by the National Geographic Society
1145 17th Street, N.W.
Washington, D.C. 20036

First printing, April 1999

"A Prologue, by the Sea," "Shorty, Slim, and the Cave Demon," and "Saddleback," have appeared under different titles and in different form in *Heart of the Land: Essays on Last Great Places,* Pantheon Books; *Princeton Alumni Weekly,* and *Preservation,* respectively. "The Night of the Whales" and "A Short Journey to the Unknown," have appeared in *The Wilson Quarterly.*

Printed in the United States of America

Library of Congress Cataloging-in-Publication Data

Warner, William W.
    Into the porcupine cave and other odysseys: adventures of an
occasional naturalist / William W. Warner.
        p.   cm.
    ISBN 0-7922-7455-5
    1. Natural history.   I. Title.
QH81.W29   1998
508—dc21   98-42055
                                                    CIP

To the memory of John Boyd,
Wymberly Coerr, and Bezal Jesudason.

Contents

~

A PROLOGUE,
BY THE SEA

~

Very little in my upbringing seems to have pointed toward a love for the world of nature, much less for writing about it. I was born and grew up in New York City in a house that was without great books, without a father, and, for some periods of the year, without a mother. In *loco patris* I had only a highly irascible step-grandfather. Col. George Washington Kavanaugh was his name, and he wanted to be known by all of it. His most frequent utterance to me, apart from constant reminders that I was no blood kin, went something like this: "Your father is a bum, your mother is running around with every gigolo in Europe, so I suppose the spring can rise no higher than its source."

So much for the Colonel, as my brother and I always

called him, and the genetic malediction he constantly laid on us. But there was one thing the Colonel did for us for which we are both eternally grateful. Come June every year he took our family, such as it was, to a place called Spring Lake, a summer resort on the New Jersey coast. Not that we especially liked the place. Our schoolmates all went "to the country" on vacations, and Spring Lake with its kiosked boardwalks, well-ordered streets, and great hotels with long porches and double rows of rocking chairs didn't seem very country to us. Reinforcing this impression was an institution known as the Bath and Tennis Club, where our contemporaries spent much of the day playing blackjack and sneaking cigarettes.

But at one end of the well-ordered streets, beyond the boardwalk and the great hotels, was an immense space. How immense I learned from my older brother, who at age nine or ten gave me my first taste for geography. "Look here," he said, showing me a world map and running his finger along the 40th parallel, "there is nothing but the Atlantic Ocean between our beach and the coast of Portugal, 4,000 miles away."

Suffice it to say that this bit of information, which was quite accurate, overwhelmed me. I soon began taking long walks along the beach, staring out at the ocean and dreaming of the day I might have a boat of my own to venture beyond the breakers and explore it. My brother shared this vision, although more in terms of a quest for better fishing.

In due course we therefore built a crude box-shaped scow of heavy pine planking, painted it red, white, and green, and proudly named it the *Rex* after the great Italian ocean liner that was at the time the largest and most luxurious ship in the transatlantic passenger service. With the help of some of our huskier friends, we grunted the *Rex* down to the beach. The chosen day was fine, with a sprightly land breeze that did much to calm the breakers. Our plan was to alternately fish and paddle down to an inlet at the south end of Spring Lake that led into a small bay known as Wreck Pond. But after we were successfully launched, our friends all laughing and cheering us on, we found the *Rex* to be something less than seaworthy and quite difficult to paddle. In fact the sprightly western breeze that had made our passage through the surf so easy was now rapidly carrying us out to sea—straight for Portugal, I could not help thinking—with a strength against which our best efforts were no match. The reader can guess what followed. Alarms were sounded, authorities were summoned, and we were rescued. "One more trick like this and I'm cutting you out of my will," the Colonel said to us when we were brought home, humiliated, by the Coast Guard.

Nevertheless, before the summer was over, my brother and I found we could explore the incongruously named Wreck Pond well enough by foot and bicycle. It was in fact what biologists call a complete estuarine system, in miniature. At its mouth was the tide-scoured inlet, constantly shifting its sandy course. Behind the inlet was a shallow bay, a labyrinth of marsh islands, and ultimately, well inland, a freshwater stream fed by a millpond bordered by pin oak and magnolia. Thanks to this complex, we could do everything from netting crabs and small fish to stalking the marsh flats looking for shorebirds, muskrat, or an occasional raccoon. We could even catch small trout up by the millpond dam, graciously provided by the New Jersey state fish hatcheries. What a relief these occasions offered from the Bath and Tennis Club; what an escape from the Colonel! Wreck Pond became our private world.

But there were other worlds to conquer, as the saying goes, and my brother and I remained eager to find them. In particular there was a large blank space on maps of the coast that we had both noticed and wondered about. It appeared as a long finger of land pointing southward, a mere ribbon of land between the Atlantic Ocean and Barnegat Bay. Most remarkably the southern part of the finger, below a cluster of closely spaced beach resorts, showed no signs of human settlement nor even a road, as far as we could tell. The blank space was called Island Beach. It had to be investigated, we agreed.

For this greater enterprise we borrowed a canoe, provisioned it with three days' worth of canned pork and beans, and left an ambiguous note concerning our intentions on the Colonel's pillow. But once again the Aeolian gods did not favor us. This time a wet east wind slammed us against the marshes of Barnegat Bay's western shore, so strongly that we found we could only gain ground by wading in the shallows and pushing and pulling the canoe. There was one bright moment in this otherwise dismal effort, however. After rounding a sharp bend in one of the marsh islands, we came upon a sheltered and relatively quiet cove. There to our amazement were four or five mink cavorting down a mud slide they had excavated in the marsh bank. Over and over they shot down the slide—head first, tail first, on their stomachs, on their backs—to splash into the water with splendid abandon. Well hidden by the tall cordgrass, we watched transfixed as the mink evidently scrambled up an underwater burrow, reappeared above on the marsh bank, shook their silvery-wet coats, and repeated the process— forever, it seemed, or for what must have been at least ten minutes. I have never forgotten the sight, nor seen another mink slide since.

We passed what seemed like a sleepless night huddled under a tump of bushes in the cordgrass, which offered little cover from intermittent rains. The next morning we set out again, very tired, under a hazy sun and on glassy, calm waters. Island Beach seemed almost in sight on the far horizon to the east, although it was hard to be sure in the haze. Just as we began to ponder the wisdom of continuing our journey, a large and official-looking motorboat with a slanted red stripe on its bow came alongside bearing instructions to take us in tow. "That does it!" the Colonel said to us two hours later when we were brought home again, humiliated but grateful, by the Coast Guard. "I'm cutting you both out of my will."

A few years later, when I was 16, I got to Island Beach. I got there in what today is known as an ORV, or off-road vehicle. But mine was quite different from current models. Mine was a splendid little ORV, in fact, for which I make no apologies. Unknown to the Colonel I had acquired a lightweight Model T Ford beach-buggy prototype with a chopped-down body, painted in salt-resistant aluminum and equipped with four enlarged wheel rims and tires, all for the sum of $50. My buggy was totally incapable of sustained driving in soft sand, having only the standard two-wheel drive, and a weak one at that. It could hardly alter the beach topography, much less charge up a sand dune. To operate it successfully on Island Beach it was necessary to travel at low tide only, along the wet and more compact swash sand of the foreshore. This meant driving along close to the surf, constantly dodging the biggest waves, in what proved to be a thoroughly exhilarating experience. One could do this, moreover, for ten glorious miles, ten miles of wind-plumed breakers rolling in from the Atlantic, ten miles with seldom another human being in sight. Sometimes there would be schools of marauding bluefish just beyond the surf, marked by sprays of small fish breaking the surface and the screams of wheeling gulls and terns. In such event I would jam on the brakes (stepping on the reverse gear pedal worked even better), grab my cane surf rod, and heave out a heavy lead squid lure as far as possible. If your cast went far enough, you got your blue. By the time you brought him in and unhooked him, you had to jump back into the buggy and race on to catch up with the fast-moving school. For a boy of 16 these were moments of pure bliss, of feeling at one with the sea and the sand.

There were other attractions. Often I would leave my fishing companions to their patient pursuits and explore the back beach. The dunes of Island Beach were low, but with steep rampartlike faces on their seaward side. Behind the ramparts were small hollows of smooth sand marked only with the delicate circular tracings made by the tips of swaying dune grass. Then came beach heather and thickets of sea myrtle, stunted cedar, holly, and scrub oak. Gain the highest point of land, perhaps no more than 20 feet above sea level, and the small world of Island Beach lay revealed before you. On the one side were the choppy waves of Barnegat Bay at its broadest, bordered by salt marsh and tidal flats that attracted great numbers of both migrant and resident shorebirds. On the other were the dunes, the white sand, and the Atlantic breakers stretching away to a seeming infinity. It was a small world, easy to comprehend, and I loved it from the beginning.

New Jersey's Island Beach is what is known to geologists as a barrier island. (The fact that it is not now an island is merely a question of time; it once was and could be again anytime after a hurricane or winter storm washes over its narrow width to create an inlet.) Barrier islands are the dominant feature of our Atlantic and Gulf Coast shorelines, and they are found there to an extent not matched elsewhere in the world. Over the years I have visited many of them and found them all as fascinating, each in their own way, as Island Beach. In the north are the high dunes of Cape Cod and the tide-swept and relatively barren Monomoy Island. In the south are the quiet groves of live oak and palmetto of the sea islands of South Carolina, rapidly being lost to development, or Georgia's Cumberland Island, mercifully spared by a combination of public and private sources. In between these is the lonely majesty of North Carolina's Hatteras Island, now part of the Cape Hatteras National Seashore. Fifty-five miles long and for the most part pencil thin, the island lies between the Atlantic Ocean and the broad expanse of Pamlico Sound. Drive down below the Cape Hatteras Lighthouse to the extreme tip or cusp of the cape (the Cape Point, as it is called, is a rapidly lengthening sand spit) and cast your eyes seaward. For as far as you can see the seas rise up in pyramidal crests and tumble against each other in wild confusion, even in a moderate breeze. But here there are no rocks or underwater reefs. Rather, what you are witnessing is the clash of the Atlantic coast's two great current systems—the cold and southward-tending Labrador Current and the warmer waters of a Gulf Stream gyre. Underneath them, extending 12 miles out to sea, are the shifting sands of the dread Diamond Shoals, known as the "graveyard of the Atlantic." So it was in the age of sail, for some 80 known shipwrecks. Little wonder the sailor's rhyme[*]:

> If the Dry Tortugas let you pass,
> Beware the Cape of Hatteras.

Little wonder, too, that in this wild setting the Hatteras Light will soon be moved back from the sea's grasp. Or that the oak frames of old ships, once buried out on the shoals, are periodically exhumed on Hatteras's retreating beach.

Not far to the north of the Outer Banks are the barrier islands of Virginia's Eastern Shore. Starting with the Chincoteague National Wildlife Refuge on Assateague Island, these islands run 80 miles south to Cape Charles at the mouth of the Chesapeake Bay. They are 11 in number counting only the larger islands, and all but two of them are protected by a combination of federal, state, and private sources. At the north is Wallops Island, home to a NASA space-tracking center, whose landlords have at least kept

---

[*] Sailing-ship captains from Gulf ports who tried a shortcut through the coral reefs that run between the Dry Tortugas and Key West, 70 miles to the east, sometimes came to grief before reaching the deep water of the Straits of Florida, where the Gulf Stream originates. Similarly, captains who elected to ride the stream's favorable current close inshore as far north as Cape Hatteras often found themselves in trouble over the Cape's notorious Diamond Shoals, in any easterly storm. Thus the rhyme.

the island off limits to visitors. At the southern extremity is Fishermans Island, a small national wildlife refuge at the tip of the Cape Charles corridor, where migrating hawks and falcons forgather in the fall before crossing the Chesapeake. In between, or at the heart of this system, are 12 islands—Smith, Myrtle, Mink, Godwin, Ship Shoal, Cobb, Little Cobb, Hog, Revel, Parramore, Cedar, and Metomkin—that comprise the Nature Conservancy's Virginia Coast Reserve. These islands and the adjoining back bay and salt marshes, totaling 35,000 acres, are a meeting ground for northern and southern plant and animal species and thus have a rich biological diversity. For this reason they have been given world-class status and designated by the United Nations as a World Biosphere Reserve. Equally important, they are the longest continuous undisturbed beachfront of our Atlantic coast.

For me the Virginia islands have long held a peculiar fascination. One reason is that getting to them is often an adventure in itself. There are no roads, bridges, or causeways to the Virginia barriers. Rather, you must go by shallow-draft boat and have some knowledge of the labyrinth of marsh creeks, tidal flats, broad bays, and deep-running ancient river courses that lie between the mainland and the outer islands. This area—the back bays, as they are sometimes called—literally pulsates with life. The mud banks of the marsh creeks come alive at low tide with *Uca pugnax*, or the feisty and well-known fiddler crabs, darting in and out of their burrows. Great blue herons or their lesser cousins wait for them at almost every bend in the creeks. Out on the broad marsh you will see marsh hawks circling the hammocks and tumps of firm land. Ospreys dive in the inlets to compete in winter with loons and mergansers. In the fall there will be huge flights of snow geese and brant numbering in the tens of thousands, not to mention the ubiquitous Canada goose and a variety of tipping and diving ducks. Out in the broader bays you will find commercial fishermen dragging for the succulent hard clams and salty oysters these waters offer in profusion. At certain low tides the oystermen will snub their boats to the channel banks, step out onto the bordering tidal flats, and take their pick of the best oysters. These same flats offer prime feeding grounds for oystercatchers and a host of other shorebirds. Willets, yellowlegs, sanderlings, turnstones, glossy ibises, whimbrels, and marbled godwits are always present in season. Other species come in astounding number. Flocks of over a thousand dunlins may be seen in winter, and an estimated 6,000 knots have been counted feeding on the larvae of blue mussels on Metomkin Island in the spring.

Summer will see large populations of black skimmers nesting on isolated sandbars, while great egrets and tricolored herons occupy their crowded nests in the shrubs and small trees of the marsh hammocks. Visitors from the south include the brown pelican, white ibis, and Wilson's plover, which nests here at the northern limit of its range.

Summertime will also see great silvery tarpon rolling through the inlets, although not in great number, and more rarely loggerhead turtles lured from Florida by warming waters. Visitors from the north include the endangered piping plover, which finds the shell fragments of undisturbed beaches much to its liking for nesting materials. Terns—Caspian, common, gull-billed, royal, and sandwich—prefer to nest on the berm of the island beaches, not far from the dune line. But the swift-flying Forster's, which can hover like a small hawk, will build its nest from the wrack of the marsh islands. Beneath the shallow bay waters are wavy meadows of sea lettuce and other aquatic plants. These underwater meadows are a favored hiding place for the tasty Atlantic blue crab, which searches them out to molt, and a nursery and juvenile growth area for a great many fish, including valuable commercial species that will return to the sea as young adults. The list of all the living treasures so carefully guarded and nourished in the lee of the barrier islands could go on.

I like best to visit Parramore Island, the largest in the Virginia Coast Reserve, in mid-October. Starting from the reserve headquarters to the south, there is only a suggestion of what is to come. After passing through narrow tidal creeks, a thin dark line begins to appear far out on the horizon. This is Hog Island, seven wind-swept miles from the mainland across the reserve's broadest bay, now dotted with small flocks of oldsquaws and buffleheads. But soon there will be the shelter of more tidal creeks and salt marshes as Parramore's mid-island forest comes into view. Overhead are the long V's of Canada geese, flying south. The first snow geese may also have arrived, and ducks are everywhere, wheeling and turning in the clear autumn sky or dropping down swiftly to marsh potholes. After landing on Parramore's bay side, one traverses a pond-studded salt marsh and enters a forest of loblolly pine, surprisingly tall for being so close to the sea. The air is cool and quiet, and the carpet of pine needles makes walking easy. An inquisitive deer may approach you, completely unafraid, as if wondering where you fit in the island's scheme of things. Migrating warblers flit overhead. But soon, very suddenly, you break out of the forest near the ruins of a Coast Guard lifesaving station. There is the ocean. And there is the beach, the broad and gently sloping beach, and the long rows of breakers rolling in from the Atlantic.

At this time of year you may want to look for the long wavy lines of scoters beating their way south just beyond the breakers. Or be on watch for the rare peregrine falcon rocketing down to Cape Charles. Or you may simply want to train your binoculars in either direction, as far as vision will carry, until there are only mirages where sand, sea, and sky come together in a common haze. To pause, that is to say, and gaze at Parramore's endless beach. There are not many like it. Pray God it may remain so.

Thinking back I sometimes wonder where or to whom one should express gratitude for the rich experience our national seashores and other coastal reserves so generously provide. In my case thanks would have to begin with New Jersey's Island Beach, scene of my boyhood awakening and still preserved by the state's Department of Environmental Protection. Or perhaps even further back to Wreck Pond, Spring Lake, and, yes, even the Colonel. It was he, after all, who drove my brother and me to those first escapes, those first new worlds of refuge. Then came bicycle trips to the New Jersey Pine Barrens, where we thrilled to the discovery of abandoned cranberry bogs, the ruins of bog-iron smelters, and ghost towns with names like Double Trouble, Mount Misery, and Hanover Furnace. Next, when we were both of lawful age for driver's licenses, we might borrow one of the Colonel's automobiles, leave another ambiguous note on his pillow, and head for the Maine woods or other more distant hideaways. With these trips came knowledge of other provinces and a much greater appreciation of nature.

Over the long years since, I have felt a strong need for more such escapes, sometimes with my brother or others, but more often alone. In either case I have always experienced the sense of wonder and well-being that nature alone seems best able to provide. It is these senses and these experiences that I hope to share with the reader to the degree possible in the pages that follow.

This being so, it is perhaps only right that I first thank the Colonel. So I will say a word to him now, in a form of address I never used in his lifetime. Namely, thank you, Grandpa, for getting me into all this. And thank you, too, Grandpa, for getting me out, in another sense, at a very critical moment. On that day long ago when my brother and I were drifting rapidly toward Portugal in the *Rex*, it was you, after all, who called the Coast Guard.

INTO THE
PORCUPINE CAVE

~

One spring day many years ago my friend Henry Buck and I found ourselves inside a small cave along with about 12 porcupines. Its entrance was also small, so small, in fact, that Henry and I had been forced to get down on our hands and knees and then wriggle through on our stomachs to get in. Now we wanted very much to get out. So, too, did the porcupines. Thus it happened that we were all standing in line, so to speak, waiting our turn. Some porcupines were ahead of us, stumbling toward a beam of light at the cave entrance. Others were behind us, rustling around with impatience.

It was not a comfortable situation. Henry Buck was ahead of me, and I was supposed to bring up the rear and keep a flashlight trained on him to guide his way out. But while I waited, I became acutely conscious of the porcupines behind me. Any one of them might decide to break for freedom and run between my legs. I knew that porcupines could not truly throw their quills, as is commonly supposed. But I also knew that they have powerfully muscled tails with thick quills that they use as their primary weapon of defense and attack. What if a porcupine chose to swat me in the leg with its tail as it passed? Worse, what might happen when I had to bend over and get on my hands and knees to get out?

It was not, as I say, a comfortable situation. How I got into it in the first place demands some explanation, I suppose. The easiest way would be to put all the blame on Henry Buck. But that would not be entirely accurate. True, Henry was the instigator of our expedition to the cave. But the more he explained his master strategy for capturing a pair of porcupines, the more I began to share some of his enthusiasm.

Then, too, there was the fact that no one else seemed willing to accompany him. At the New England preparatory school we attended at the time, he was known as Frank "Bring-'Em-Back-Alive" Buck, after the legendary Oklahoma Indian of the same name who was then gaining world renown for his daring captures of lions, tigers, and other animals for zoos and the Ringling Bros. and Barnum & Bailey Circus. Indeed, Henry was himself becoming something of a legend at our school. He had captured a huge snapping turtle in the school pond with his bare hands. He had forced woodchucks out of their burrows with smoke bombs and fed mice to a corn snake hidden in a shoebox in his room. And sometimes, just for a prank, he might anoint the pulpit in the school chapel with skunk oil shortly before the Sunday service.

Still, the proposed porcupine expedition bespoke more interest and seriousness of purpose than most of Henry's exploits. In the autumn, or three months ahead of time, he had sent for the appropriate U.S. Geological Survey quadrangle maps and set out in search of the cave, the exact location of which was supposed to be known only to the school's upperclassmen. For my part I convinced my older brother, who had visited the cave before during his junior year, to give us some clues to its whereabouts. Between Henry Buck's survey and my brother's help we were fairly certain we knew where to go.

We were to wait, however, until the following spring. As Henry saw it, there was no point in going in the fall. The porcupines could still be anywhere in the woods; they would not den up in the cave until snows were deep and temperatures well below freezing. The ideal time, Henry insisted, was early spring, when the porcupines might still be shaking off the effects of a long winter's sleep. In the interim we would build a cage in the basement of our dormitory. Then when the time came, all we needed to do was capture a male and a female porcupine. Later in the spring they were bound to get the mating urge, Henry explained to me with a salacious grin, and that would surely be something to observe. The more we thought of how porcupines managed to copulate without hurting themselves, the more interest the trip took on for both of us. There was also the fact that Henry had been unable to find any descriptions or even references to porcupine mating in the school library. Perhaps the phenomenon had never really been observed, we began to think. Yes, it was just possible that we would be making a signal contribution to the biological sciences!

The winter months were spent in obtaining materials for the cage and building it—little by little, that is to say, lest our grand design become widely known. Secrecy was necessary because the school had strict rules against keeping pets or any form of animal life. To this end Henry had suborned the dormitory janitor, a dour northern Italian who liked Henry's jokes and the sour fruit balls he gave him.

Finally, around the middle of March, Henry announced the great moment to launch our experiment was at hand. The day we chose was a brilliant Saturday, with blue skies and a bright sun beating down on a thick cover of granular snow—ideal maple-sugar weather in northern New England. The protective gear we thought necessary for struggling with porcupines filled one mountaineering rucksack. In it were ice hockey knee-and-shin guards, a baseball catcher's chest protector, several pairs of gloves suitable for layering, a double-lined burlap bag, and two fencing masks, which we later discarded because they seemed to limit our visibility. More important, perhaps, was a late-model flashlight that Henry had bought at Abercrombie and Fitch's famed New York store. It was self-generating, meaning the harder you pumped and squeezed its mechanical handle the brighter it shone. It was to prove our most critical piece of equipment, in more ways than one.

We started off in good spirits, taking turns carrying the rucksack as we slogged through the granular snow. After about an hour we passed over Berry Hill, a school landmark, and descended into a steep valley. While climbing the opposite slope, Henry Buck stopped frequently to inspect bark scratchings on beech and maple trees.

"We're on the trail," Henry proclaimed triumphantly. "Porcupines are bark eaters and those are porcupine scratches."

After climbing the slope for another 300 feet of elevation, he turned around, told me to be very quiet, and pointed to a small opening in a rocky outcrop. Immediately beneath it was a fan of pellet-shaped dung.

"That's porcupine scat," Henry whispered. "I knew we would find it. This is it!"

"This is what?" I asked, my voice betraying serious misgivings.

This was the cave, no doubt about it, Henry insisted. Some of the world's largest caves had very small entrances, he wanted me to know. There was nothing for it but to get down on our hands and knees and have a look inside.

With some reluctance I put on my protective gear and prepared to follow Henry Buck. We crawled in, one by one, cautiously and as silently as possible. Once inside we found that if we remained close together in one particular spot, there was just enough height to stand up. What confronted us was not so much a cave but rather a chamber formed by two large slabs of rock. One was the floor of the chamber; it sloped upward for about 15 yards at an angle of 45 degrees. The other was the ceiling, which sloped downward at a lesser angle to meet it. Where the two met, our self-generating flashlight revealed some dark masses in what looked like animal shapes. They were the porcupines, curled up in a long row and seemingly fast asleep.

"Look!" said Henry in a low voice. "They're in a state of hibernation."

After a whispered argument on strategy Henry said he was going to climb up the slope in the farthest reaches of the cave to one side of where the porcupines were and "pick one off from behind," as he expressed it. I was to stand fast, training the light on him and holding the double-lined burlap bag into which he would drop his captured specimen. When I protested that it would be extremely difficult to perform both functions simultaneously, he did not listen. He was already on his way, climbing up the slope.

"Keep that light on me, you hear!" he said in parting.

I squeezed and pumped the Abercrombie & Fitch flashlight

as fast as I could, until it began to make a high-pitched whine. Better said, a *loud* and high-pitched whine, the very volume of which made me nervous lest it disturb the hibernating porcupines. In fact when I trained the beam on them a moment later, there were small dots of reflected light from what I presumed to be their open eyes. They seemed to be coming out of their long winter's sleep rather quickly, I thought to myself.

"Goddamit, keep the light on me," Henry Buck shouted.

A few seconds later there was no more question about it. Henry was halfway up the cave's sloping floor, and already the porcupines were on the move, rustling about in every direction.

"They're not hibernating anymore," I yelled, giving voice to what was all too obvious. "Let's get out of here."

Porcupines, the reader should know, do not in fact hibernate. It is true that they seek shelter in winter dens, but they also go out to forage for bark or twigs, usually at night. Rocky outcroppings or crevices are much favored for winter dens, but tree branches or hollow logs will do in a pinch. A rock chamber of the size we encountered is a veritable porcupine Grand Hotel and rather rare. So, too, are communally shared dens.

But such details of porcupine habitat and seasonal rounds were far from our minds as the scene inside the cave rapidly approached bedlam.

"Goddamit, Warner, the light, the light!" Henry shouted.

"They're all down here running through my legs," I shouted back, in what was only a slight exaggeration. "Let's get out of here."

"I'm coming down," Henry now yelled. "For Chris'sakes keep the light on me!"

I do not clearly remember everything that followed. I know that at least one porcupine brushed my leg. Two or more were behind me, rearing up with erectile quills. I kept pumping the Abercrombie lantern with all my strength. For the most part I kept it trained on Henry in his downward progress. But whenever I sensed a porcupine was close to me, I would swing the beam down around my feet. Henry cursed every time I did this. Eventually, or after what seemed a very long time, he slipped on some fresh porcupine droppings and slid to a stop in front of me. After a volley of oaths we prepared to get out.

Again, very few of the events that followed are clear in my mind. But I do remember suddenly standing outside, squinting in the brilliant sun and feeling immensely relieved that our ordeal was over.

My sense of relief, however, soon proved premature. Three or four porcupines shuffled away from us in the snow, seemingly as blinded as we were by the sudden flood of light. Before I could object, Henry Buck yelled at me to follow him closely with the bag open as he half-ran and half-stumbled in pursuit of the porcupines. He then made a desperate lunge for the nearest one, grabbed it by the tail before it had a chance to raise its quills, and literally threw it at me just as I opened the bag. I caught it, in a manner of speaking, but the weight of the porcupine and the force of Henry's toss caught me off balance and caused me to tumble backward in the snow. (Adult porcupines weigh between 8 to 15 pounds, according to sex, with some males going as high as 20.) When I regained a measure of composure, I noticed a spray of quills on the left sleeve of my wool jacket. I also noticed that Henry had somehow managed to come to my aid and tie off the top of the double burlap bag. From within it came a harsh cacophony of squawks and screeches.

"Look!" said Henry. "There's another one up in that little tree." Sure enough, a disoriented porcupine had climbed a young sapling that was standing alone in a clearing, isolated from any other trees.

Henry then told me he would shake the tree while I held the bag. I protested, presenting my quill-studded sleeve as mute testimony to the perils of bag holding. I would shake the tree, I insisted, and he could hold the bag. Henry grumbled, but said he would do it; it was no big thing.

The second capture was relatively easy. After a few vigorous shakes, the porcupine let loose of the sapling and tried to jump to freedom. But Frank "Bring-'Em-Back-Alive"

Buck was ready and caught it neatly in the bag. The first porcupine squealed loudly in protest.

Porcupines like to climb trees. Not just for escape or defense, but also for food, rest, and sleep. They will eat the inner bark of a number of trees and also such varied fare as hemlock needles, acorns, apples, and grasses. Surprisingly, for animals that spend most of their waking hours high up in trees, porcupines are prone to fall to the ground with some frequency. This is probably due to their predilection for "niptwigging," or biting off leafy twigs near the end of branches and then retreating to a more secure point to eat the leaves. Since the choicest niptwigs are often far out on the branches, the porcupines may crawl out too far for their own good. The branch snaps and the porcupines fall. Fortunately, autopsies have shown that their broken bones seem to knit rather well. And almost no other animal will dare to attack a porcupine, even when it is hurt and forced to remain on the ground during its recovery period.

As we prepared to start back to school, I was struck with the thought that after all our efforts we might not have caught a male and female. But I wanted no more of porcupine catching and made no mention of it. Besides, truth to say, neither Henry Buck nor I knew how to tell the difference.

A few trial lifts of the now heavy bag convinced us we

could not carry it slung over our shoulders, to say nothing of the possibility of being jabbed by protruding quills. Henry therefore laboriously chopped down and trimmed a sapling with a small ax he had brought along for just such a contingency. We then hung the bag in the middle of the sapling and each shouldered an end of it.

Thus we set off with the porcupine-filled bag swaying and bouncing on the limber sapling. From time to time as we trudged along in the melting snow, one or the other of the two porcupines emitted a series of pathetic squeaks. They seemed to carry a weary note of resignation, of knowledge that further struggle was useless. Or, I wondered, could it be that one porcupine was sticking its quills into the other? Was this possible? I began to feel waves of remorse.

Porcupines, as I later learned, can and do leave quills in one another. The occasions, however, are rare and most often associated with territorial and mating conflicts. Typically two males will begin by facing off and clacking their teeth, as do wolves and certain other mammals. If this tactic does not repel the interloper, the resident male will attack, trying to drive his tail quills into his opponent's face. Usually both succeed in doing so in the melee that follows, which is accompanied by what one observer has called "loud and unearthly screams." In other encounters, or porcupines versus other species, porcupines do not need to drive their quills into their opponent. More often than not the attacker will be impaled on the porcupine's quills by the force of his or her own momentum. The quills detach easily and the attacker retreats in pain.

We stumbled on, stopping more frequently for rest. The late afternoon sun went down as we passed over Berry Hill, and the streams and rivulets of melting snow became quiet. As the air grew much cooler, our nostrils began to tingle with a faint reminder that winter was not quite over. Distressing squeaks continued to come from inside the double burlap bag, and I could not help thinking once again that the porcupines were wounding each other with their quills. I hoped we would reach school before dark.

An adult porcupine is equipped with approximately 30,000 barbed quills. The quills of the head, neck, and rump are the longest. They measure about four inches and are strikingly white in color, tipped with black. The quills of the tail are black on the tail's upper surface but white along its sides. These tail quills are noticeably shorter but the most dangerous. A porcupine can drive them so hard that they disappear entirely under a victim's skin. (And sometimes reappear at a different point from the entry a few days later.) Scientists believe the porcupine's white-and-black quills seen from a distance serve as a potent warning signal to other animals, much like a skunk's black-and-white fur pattern. Dog owners, however, will probably not agree. Nor with the fact that porcupine tail and back quills have a film of grease which makes entry easier and presumably less painful. But as Dr. Uldis Roze of Queens College, an expert in the study of porcupines, has recently discovered, this same grease has strong antibiotic properties. So much so, in fact, that infections from quill wounds are extremely rare. Such are nature's little grace notes.

It was indeed dark by the time we reached the school grounds, approaching quietly through the woods. All the lights in our dormitory windows shone brilliantly, except Henry's and mine, which were dark and therefore stood out like missing teeth. As yet, however, we were not in any trouble. It was Saturday, after all. This meant that there was no evening study hall and thus time enough to make supper, the first occasion when our absence would be noted. Henry put down his end of the sapling, walked to the road at the edge of the woods, and looked up and down the open field between us and our dormitory.

"Okay, the coast is clear," he whispered conspiratorially. "Let's make a run for it."

Making a run for it, however, proved much easier said than done. If we ran or jogged out of step, the bag hanging from the limber sapling danced such an erratic jig that it was difficult to keep our footing. In the rare moments when we did jog in step, it bounced up and down to such heights that I thought it might fly off on its own orbit. By now, too, loud screeches, not pathetic squeaks, came from inside the bag.

Presently we gained the back door of the dormitory, out of breath and seen only by one classmate whom neither of us knew very well.

"One word about this and you're dead," Henry hissed at him as we rushed the porcupines down to their basement cage.

On Sunday we proudly recounted the previous day's adventures to a few of our closest friends, swore them to secrecy, and invited them down to the basement to see the porcupines. Henry watched the pair closely for most of the day looking for signs of amorous intent or, if not, at least a measure of compatibility. But as far as I could see, their behavior suggested just the opposite or, if not hostility, at least mutual annoyance with each other. One porcupine, the smaller of the two, repeatedly climbed the wire mesh of the cage. The other looked at him (or her?) with suspicion, occasionally giving out a loud squawk. I told Henry it might still be a little early for our porcupines to have the mating urge. Henry, who was now convinced we had a male and a female, agreed. Time alone will tell, he said; time alone will tell.

Time, though, was to be the one missing element in our great contribution to science. On Monday morning, when the entire middle- and upper-school student bodies had gathered in what was called the big study hall for the daily reports and announcements, Henry and I received one of the greater shocks of our younger years.

After reading the list of demerits incurred during the weekend for minor offenses, the school's vice-rector made a startling announcement. "Buck and Warner Second," he solemnly intoned, "proceed to the rectory immediately following reports."

There could be no mistake. I was "Warner Second" by virtue of having an older brother in the senior class, and the joint naming of Henry and myself meant only one thing. We had been betrayed, as Henry chose to put it. Somehow or other, word of our escapade had gotten out. Now we almost certainly faced the Red List, the school's most severe punishment short of expulsion, which meant extra study-hall periods in what was already a demanding daily class and study-hall schedule.

It was as we expected. The rector, a stern New England cleric and headmaster typical of a generation long passed, began by saying that Mr. McCreary, the science teacher, had already told him of our progress in biology and that he, the rector, did not want to stand in the way of our lively interest in the natural world. But we certainly knew the school's regulations against keeping animals of any kind. And we certainly knew full well that a wild animal's place was not in the furnace room of a basement.

"Yes, gentlemen, you of all students should know that wild animals are God's most pure and innocent creations," the rector concluded. "They are poor dumb beasts, to be sure, without man's higher qualities. But they are born free of sin, born to roam freely in the forest, to partake of nature's bounty, and to rest in nature's green and leafy bower."

The rector sat back in his chair, seemingly pleased with his own eloquence, and waited for us to reply. When we did not, he told us that there was simply no excuse for what we had done. In spite of our knowledge and appreciation of God's kingdom, we had cruelly treated some of his most innocent servants. In spite of our awareness of the school's regulations, we had deliberately flaunted them. Really, we had left him no choice in the matter. We were to be placed on the Red List for two months, starting that afternoon, by which time also we were to release the porcupines into what he called the nearest suitable habitat.

In the short interval between the Red List afternoon and evening study halls we carried our cage to the woods behind our dormitory and opened its door to set the porcupines free. At first they seemed hesitant to reenter their natural world, as though the cage had come to mean a form of relative security. But after we momentarily hid from their sight, they climbed out and shuffled off in their steady side-to-side gait. I was sorry not to have had more of an opportunity to observe them, of course. But something in the way they walked away together affected me. By now I had come to believe the larger of the pair was a healthy male and the smaller, a female, just as Henry Buck did. Was it possible that the ordeals of capture and brief captivity had brought them together? I hoped so. In any case I wished them well.

Porcupines need all the friends they can get. They go about minding their own business, secure in their armor of quills, never bothering much less purposely attacking another species of animal. Yet they have been shot, trapped, poisoned, and run over in astounding numbers. Until very recently certain New England states paid out bounties of $90,000 to $100,000 a year for porcupine snouts, at 50 cents a snout, all because of the lumber industry's exaggerated claim that porcupine bark scratching and niptwigging significantly damaged their trees. Another cause for the porcupines' decline is their craving for salt. This craving is so intense that it leads them to woodland houses, where they will patiently gnaw away at any plywood within their reach for its salt content. (Or to the urine-impregnated wood of outhouses, as a friend of mine once discovered to his complete surprise.) The porcupines' salt drive also draws them to roads and highways, where they feast on rock salt and may be run over. Then, too, there are angry dog owners and persons who are quite simply afraid of porcupines and don't want them around. Man, in short, has become the porcupine's single greatest enemy.

In the days that followed some of our classmates went out of their way to console us or tell us they thought our punishment was too severe. Many more, however, pestered us with questions or comments, some serious and others sarcastic. Had we really witnessed porcupine mating? Or, tell us, wasn't it a prick-ly affair? At first Henry did not wish to admit that we had failed in our attempt to observe the phenomenon and therefore gave temporizing answers.

"Oh, yes, you have to be around for a long time to see them do it," he would say. "It takes a lot of patience to catch them in the act." These answers, we would both learn much later, had far more truth than either of us ever imagined at the time.

Female porcupines are in heat for only 8 to 12 hours in the course of a year. Remarkably, this has not proved a serious impediment to procreation mainly because the female emits a vaginal secretion that, mixed with her urine, becomes a strong attractant to any and all males in her general vicinity. The randy males for their part exhibit a commendable patience. They will follow the female's secretion for as long as a week, constantly sniffing it to judge how long it may be before her estrus. During all this time, moreover, the male who eventually wins out will have to fight off a number of suitors in vicious battles. Then, when he first draws near to his intended, he may suffer frequent and sometimes nasty tail-swatting rejections. Finally, when the magic moment of acceptance comes, he will perform a bizarre act shared only by certain other rodents. Professor Roze has so described it: "The male approaches on his hind legs and tail, grunting in a low tone. His penis springs erect. He then becomes a urine cannon, squirting high-pressure jets of urine at the female." If the female remains in a receptive mood after her shower, he will find her with her hind quarters raised and her tail curved out of the way. "He can now penetrate without fear of impalement," Professor Roze concludes.

When Henry and I returned after Easter vacation, we found that our porcupine escapade had reached almost mythic proportions. The questions therefore continued. How did we catch the porcupines? What did the rector say about it? What would we go after next? Didn't the porcupines hurt themselves in mating? Had we really seen it?

By this time Henry Buck told me he was tired of dissembling. But on the other hand he still could not bring himself to admit that we had not seen the act, as he chose to call it, and thus disappoint his listeners. Rather, he would give them an answer, an answer to think about.

"Oh, yes, it's incredible," he now replied. "You could say that the male has to be very careful. It's done with extreme caution."

And that, perhaps, is the best short description of the great natural phenomenon we had failed to observe.

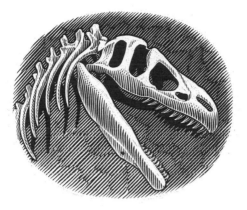

SHORTY, SLIM, AND
THE CAVE DEMON

~

In July 1941 my friend John Boyd and I drove across the
continent in an aging Packard convertible. Jutting out
from the rear of the car through its zippered Plexiglass
panel were a pair of skis. On the cramped back seat on top
of a disorderly pile of luggage was a butterfly net. The net
belonged to Boyd, an accomplished lepidopterist who liked
to keep it at the ready at all times. The skis were mine. I
hoped to use them on the slopes of Mount Lassen in northern California, a semiquiescent volcano known for its long-
lasting summer snowfields. Displayed as they were, the
skis provoked a running commentary from truck drivers
and other motorists as we drove through the heat of the
American heartland. "Where you going, buddy boy, the

North Pole?" some asked. "Hey, nutso, it's still six months until Christmas," others said, less charitably.

But neither skiing nor butterfly collecting was the reason for our journey. Rather, our ultimate destination was a boulder-strewn mesa in the desert of central Utah about 250 miles south and east of Salt Lake City. Although no one suspected it at the time, the slopes of this mesa contained a spectacular concentration of fossilized dinosaur bones from the Morrison formation of the late Jurassic period. What was known, at least to a handful of local ranchers, was that some large pieces of bone might occasionally be found weathering out of the soft limestone near the mesa's base. But it was not until Lee Stokes, a native of the nearby village of Cleveland, Utah, came to Princeton University as a graduate student that major scientific interest in the site began to take shape. Stokes asked his thesis adviser, the late Professor Glenn L. Jepsen, why the otherwise well provided Natural History Museum in Princeton's Guyot Hall had no dinosaur. "They are a little too rich for our blood," Jepsen answered, as Stokes remembers it, adding that $50,000 was then the going price for dinosaurs. Stokes, a frugal Mormon with a strong work ethic, convinced Jepsen that he might get a dinosaur out of his home grounds for far less.

After some promising exploratory digs in 1939 and 1940, Malcolm Lloyd, a Philadelphia lawyer and Princeton alumnus with a strong interest in paleontology, provided funds for what promised to be a full-scale excavation in the summer of 1941. John Boyd and I were the two undergraduates asked to participate.

First on our itinerary, however, was the planned visit to Mount Lassen Volcanic National Park, since I was concerned that its celebrated summer snows might not last very long into the month of July. I need not have worried. We arrived to find that the road through the higher parts of the park had been cleared of snow only a week before, just in time for Fourth of July visitors. To cross the higher sections, in fact, it was necessary to drive in one-way convoys escorted by park rangers through walls of snow nine or ten feet high. At intervals along the way niches had been carved out of the snow walls, where two or three cars might park. Here the Park Service had provided crude wooden ladders for anyone who wanted to climb up to the snowfield. Getting up the ladders burdened with skis and poles was not easy, but once on top the balancing act was well worth the effort. There to behold was an unobstructed view of Lassen's peak and upper slopes in all their summer glory, blindingly white against a sky of cobalt blue.

We passed some remarkably pleasant days as the sole occupants of a public campground at Lake Manzanita, near the park's northern limits, an idyllic situation that would be impossible to duplicate with today's crowds. With the whole mountain to myself I skied happily over sun-pocked snow, which at certain times of the day presented an ideal spring surface. John, who did not ski, was for the most part content to collect butterflies at the lower elevations in the lakeside woods near where we had pitched our tent. Although we had taken a number of trips together, I had not before seen John pursue his butterflies. The manner in which he captured them surprised me. Not for him was the bounding chase with an outstretched net that is the effete popular image of the butterfly collector. Rather, John, who was tall and lean and walked at a fast clip, might suddenly swoop his net through the air with a deft circular motion, catch an unsuspecting butterfly, fold over the hoop of the net to prevent its escape, and gently pop the butt end of the netting into a cyanide jar. It was as though the butterfly had simply been subtracted from the atmosphere. At one moment it was fluttering brightly through the woods; at the next it was lying inertly in a cyanide jar. In fact John's flawless technique, not to mention his devotion to science, had already won him some global recognition in the world of lepidopterists. At the age of 20 he had the honor of describing and naming a new species, *Appias drusilla* Boyd. (Unfortunately, however, John's butterfly has since been synonymized to *Glaucopsyche lygbamus* Doubleday, which means that one Doubleday had previously described what later proved to be the same species, and that although you may still use John's more mellifluous *Appias drusilla,* you will not be considered au courant unless you go with Professor Doubleday's unhappy choice.)

After three or four days at Lassen we began the long drive

to Utah. We passed the time by guessing at license plates from a distance or addressing each other in mock cowboy talk in which John became Slim and I was Shorty. ("Well I'll be hornswoggled, if that ain't a sight!" was one of John's favorite utterances, as I remember it.) Our one major stop en route was in Nevada, then the only place in the country with statewide legalized gambling, or more particularly, Harold's Casino in Reno. We had seen billboards proclaiming "Harold's or Bust! Only 1,465 Miles Ahead!" starting somewhere west of St. Louis and continuing at intervals across the rest of the continent. No doubt about it, such an institution had to be visited, we decided. We therefore detoured slightly to the center of Reno and made directly for Harold's. Striding past the slot machines and roulette wheels in our best western gait, we opted for a blackjack table. This was the one game, better known as 21 in the East, which we knew how to play.

Or so we thought. Instead we were to suffer the ultimate indignity of being banished from the table after one round. The dealer, as it turned out, had signaled to a perky young lady dressed in an imitation buckskin skirt, rodeo boots, and an oversize Stetson, who proved to be Harold's official gambling instructress. Very politely, she took us aside to explain that the game was played fast in the West and without any talk. (We had yelled "hit me again" or "standing pat," much to the astonishment of the other players, instead of scratching the green baize for another card or sliding our hands under our silver dollars to stand pat.) Perhaps we would like to try our hand at roulette, the instructress suggested. The game was easy, there were interesting variations, and the stakes weren't so high. We thanked her but declined. Instead we repaired to the nearest bar to soothe our ruffled spirits. I suggested we might do better to investigate Nevada's other great legalized distraction. Reckon so, Shorty. Reckon so, agreed Slim.

Two weary days later we arrived at the excavation site. There to greet us were Professor Glenn Jepsen, Lee Stokes, Malcolm Lloyd, and two younger persons, one of whom was Grant Stokes, Lee's younger brother, and the other, his friend Don Hansen, son of the chairman of the Department of Geology at Brigham Young University. John Boyd and I were shown to a huge sandstone boulder with a pronounced overhanging edge. Jep, as we took to calling Professor Jepsen, told us this was the ideal place to pitch our tent. Thanks to the overhang, the tent would be completely shaded from the fierce afternoon sun. Already in place were a large steel drum of drinking water and a hook to hang our flaxen water bag. (In antebellum days travelers and campers often used flaxen bags to cool water; the water would leak through the flax just enough to keep the outside of the bag covered with a film of moisture, which then evaporated in any kind of breeze, thus cooling the water inside.) There was also plenty of shaded space to store our canned foods and drinks, Jep told us. He wanted us to be as comfortable as possible, he explained, because we were to be the around-the-clock guardians of the site. This way the Stokes brothers and Don Hansen could go home to Cleveland every night, while he and Malcolm Lloyd would make a longer commute in a pickup truck from the Mission Tourist Cottages in Price.

That evening, left to ourselves, John and I surveyed our new home. My first impression of the great sheltering rock was one of impermanence. It seemed to be balancing precariously on a rather small base, as though it might be dislodged by the slightest tremor. John said, no, you could see the boulder was well grounded and had probably stayed the way it was for millennia. But then again we could hardly ignore the jumble of rocks that cascaded down the slopes of the mesa looming over us. Each was as big, or almost as big, as our home boulder and made of exactly the same sandstone. It required no great powers of deduction to determine where they had come from. Close to the top of the mesa a hundred feet above us was a long ridge of this same sandstone. There it perched, like a brittle tabletop, over the softer Morrison limestone.

The sight that greeted us the next morning on our first day of work was not what I had expected. Before us was a 30-by-40 foot pit excavated down to two levels. At the upper level, about three feet from the top, Grant Stokes and Don Hansen hacked away at the soft rock with light pickaxes and geologist hammers. At the lower level, about six feet from the top, Jep, Lee Stokes, and Malcolm Lloyd sat or worked on their hands and knees with such hand tools as chisels, ice picks, mason's trowels, and small paint brushes. Around each of them were encircling clusters of dinosaur bones, dark gray or black against the off-white of the Morrison limestone. I had half-expected to see great numbers of partly concealed bone fragments weathering out of the Morrison, which we would have to fit and glue together like jigsaw puzzle pieces and then ship off with their surrounding rock matrix in plaster of paris mummies for later extraction and analysis under laboratory conditions. That is what vertebrate paleontologists did, I thought, or what I had seen Roy Chapman Andrews do in newsreels of his Gobi Desert expedition.

But here instead were fossil bones of many kinds—vertebrae, femora, a large sacrum, ulnae, pieces of skull—plain to see and almost ready for the taking. Often Professor Jep and the others needed only to tap gently with an awl or chisel to remove whole or slightly broken bones. As I was soon to discover, these bones were heavy and smooth to the touch. Wet or painted with shellac, they glistened a dark black in the sun.

Vertebrate fossils, it must be emphasized, are not always so easy to come by. Quite often paleontologists have to contend with dinosaur bones that are poorly mineralized and therefore in a more delicate state. But this was not the case in the Cleveland quarry, as we began to call the pit. All the

Cleveland quarry bones were well preserved by a process formerly known as replacement—permineralization is now the preferred term—whereby minerals carried in underground water penetrate the bone pores and mineralize, or literally petrify, the original bone composition. In the case of the Cleveland quarry bones, the principal impregnating mineral was calcium carbonate with lesser amounts of zircon, quartz, and hematite—to which also add uranium, fortunately in a very small amount. Fortunately, that is, because had there been more, all the dinosaur remains would have been lost to the uranium mines that fuel atomic reactors, as has happened at other Morrison locations in Utah and Colorado.

Professor Jep explained to us that John and I were to open up a new section of the quarry, as Grant Stokes and Don Hansen were already doing. This meant pickaxing about two feet of overlying rock and carting it away in wheelbarrows, an exercise known as "removing the overburden," common to all archeological and paleontological digs. After reaching a depth of two feet, Jep insisted that we get on our hands and knees and chip away, using the chisels and awls with great care, until the fossil-bearing layer was reached. To do otherwise, he said, would be to risk destruction of priceless and perhaps yet unknown evidence of life in the long ago past.

By mid-afternoon we had cleared a significant portion of the area assigned to us, and Jep had allowed us to search out and remove any small whole bones we encountered, all the while watching us, I suspected, out of the corner of his eye. Searching, however, was hardly the right term. Fossil bones or parts of bones appeared to be everywhere, mixed in a remarkable density and disorder. But even with such a wealth of opportunity John seemed to have a knack for uncovering more interesting material than I did. That first afternoon, if memory serves, he came upon part of a large jawbone with all its teeth intact, a find that brought Jep and Lee Stokes over for an inspection; my first find, by contrast, was the better part of a rib bone. True, it was not whole, and one of many of its kind, yet I gloried in it. Here it was in my hand, a beautiful object, really, over 145 million years old.

The next day John and I began clearing a new section with gusto. Too much gusto on my part, in fact, for I soon swung my pickax too far down into the fossil-bearing rock. With one resounding chunk of the ax—I remember it so clearly—I dislodged the metatarsal bone of a small carnivorous dinosaur and sent it flying across the quarry close to Malcolm Lloyd's head. It was a nice-looking bone, dark black and just the right size for a large dog, I remember thinking, and it hit the opposite wall of the quarry with a loud clatter. Happily, it remained essentially undamaged. Nevertheless this was a serious malefaction in Jep's book. Always a hard taskmaster, he sentenced me to removing overburden for the remainder of that day and all of the next. To do so I had to shovel a wheelbarrow chock full of the waste rock we had removed, wheel it up an earthen ramp at one side of the quarry, and then down a dry gully to a dump site some 50 yards away. At first I went through the motions with a kind of madcap zest, charging full tilt up the ramp and then barely controlling the wheelbarrow as it careened down to the dump. But the second day, with the temperature climbing over 100°F, I found little joy in my humbling task. John, however, tried to cheer me with consoling words between each trip. "Here, old pardner," he would say. "Have a drink of this delicious warm lemonade."

After my return to the excavating team, properly penitent, the days settled into an agreeable routine. Professor Jep continually busied himself numbering bones and plotting their location and relative positions as they were found in the quarry floor on a large master chart. Malcolm Lloyd, who at the time was 67 years old, was a model of patience. He might sit for an hour or more in one place, wearing a white, round-brimmed tennis hat as his only protection from the sun, while he cautiously reassembled fragments of broken bone. Lee Stokes, his brother Grant, and Don Hansen, all of whom had previous experience at the site, worked with what can only be described as professional skill. Still, there was more than enough for John and me to share in the finds. Only when we came across what seemed to be parts of a larger body unit—a pelvis, a skull, a leg, for example—did we stop and ask for help. Occasionally, in such cases, the classic technique of plaster of paris encasement proved necessary. Of special interest to Professor Jep and Lee Stokes were some more well preserved mandibles, much like the one John had found on our first day, with all their teeth in place. Such complete jawbones were rare, Jep told us, and might provide new light on dinosaurian tooth growth and replacement.

In the late afternoon, after the others had departed, John and I would typically drink warm beer while we decided what new mixtures of canned goods we might concoct for supper. The temptation to stand under the flaxen bag and douse ourselves with cool water was always in the back of our minds, since by day's end we were usually hot, dry, and tired. But we resisted. Our water supply simply would not allow such nonessential use. In any event, as the afternoon wore down into evening, our home-under-the-rock became agreeably cool. By evening, too, the harsh and glaring landscape of the mesa's rockslide became magically tinted with shades of rose and ocher. The hot winds of the day died down and an absolute silence, the special silence of desert places, enveloped us. We usually slept peacefully.

As the excavation progressed, Jep became more and more convinced that we were witness to a dinosaur burial ground where titans of the late Jurassic had been trapped in considerable numbers and forced to fight to the finish. There were bones of brontosaurs and other of the giant plant-eaters; there were also bones of the meat-eaters much like the great *Tyrannosaurus*. All were commingled, in a rather puzzling manner. The remains of the carnivores outnumbered those of the herbivores by more than two to one, which Jep told us was exactly the opposite of what was to be found in the other Morrison deposits in Utah and Colorado. Prominent among the former was a fierce-looking flesh-eater, then known as *Antrodemus*, with a large head and long teeth. Then, too, as I remember it, many of the bones of these carnivores were whole and undamaged, whereas those of the scarcer herbivores tended more to be broken or fragmented.

This much evidence led Jep and Lee Stokes to believe the quarry site might have been a soft area, or sinkhole, in the mud bottom of a lake. From the stratigraphy of the area it was known that a vast floodplain crisscrossed by meandering rivers and dotted with shallow lakes extended over all the Morrison sites and beyond, from Utah east to Colorado and New Mexico and north to Canada. It was also generally known that the late Jurassic was a relatively dry period, although how dry, or the general nature of the climate, will probably always be a matter of discussion among geologists and climatologists. If these factors were correct, it was easy to imagine a scenario in which a water-loving plant-eater like the giant *Camarasaurus* prowled the plain in search of gradually shrinking lakes and ponds. Given a patch of soft mud bottom, *Camarasaurus* and his kin would have been the first to be mired. Only a few of these huge animals, bellowing in rage as they struggled to be free, would be enough to attract fast-running bipedal carnivores. Enter the sharp-toothed *Antrodemus*, in numbers.

I have always imagined the end of this scenario as a dreadful scene, a kind of dinosaurian Götterdämmerung. First there would be the dragonlike hiss of the carnivores as they sprang into action. Then would come roars of pain and the snap of broken bones as the attackers tore into their easy prey, after which they themselves would begin to sink. More of their kind would then hear their anguished calls and have no hesitation in pouncing on their unfortunate fellows. There all would remain, their feet stuck firmly in the mud, with their bloody heads and necks weaving back and forth in a fateful duel, like wounded gladiators. Until, finally, all was quiet and pterodactyls flew overhead to peer at their rotting flesh. And, much later, seas invaded the plain to cover them with a tombstone of shale.

How much of this scenario might prove true through further digging was something John and I did not stay to witness. After about three weeks Jep took us to Fossil, Wyoming, a whistle-stop in the southwestern corner of the state that has since disappeared from most road maps. Here we would experience a different kind of field work, Jep explained, with a formation known as the Green River shale. This was a light-colored shale from an Eocene lake bottom, fine grained and oil bearing, which contained many beautifully preserved fossil fish as well as some reptiles and plants. The site was high up on a hill and delightfully cool, the shale could easily be tapped off along its horizontal bedding planes, and the fish it contained could be cut out and framed to hang like pictures on a wall.

Following a week of this relatively pleasurable work John and I stuffed some fossil fish Jep had let us keep, my skis, John's butterfly-collecting gear, assorted bric-a-brac, and some newly purchased cowboy jeans into the back of the Packard convertible and started the long drive home. September saw us back at Princeton as members of the junior class. Professor Jepsen was already hard at work sorting and tallying the results of the summer's dig. In the graduate department, Lee Stokes was writing an article for *Science* magazine announcing that a new quarry from the Morrison formation of Utah contained "a large deposit of well-preserved dinosaur bones, heretofore undescribed." There was already enough material, he concluded, to mount a composite skeleton of *Antrodemus*.

John and I pursued our carefree undergraduate careers through the autumn, that best of all seasons at Princeton. As geology majors we were happy to be done with required courses and could now take the departmental subjects we most wanted. Then, too, there were the seasonal joys of football games, marching bands, club parties, and lazy Sundays for drinking milk punches or strolling under the

elms of Prospect Street. But then on one such Sunday—
a gray Sunday when fall was fast giving way to early
winter—we heard reports of a Japanese attack on Pearl
Harbor. We knew right away that all our lives would be
irrevocably altered.

Soon thereafter the university administration announced
an accelerated term schedule. There would be no summer
vacation. We, the juniors, could plan to graduate the following winter instead of the customary June commencement.

On the appointed day, or on February 3, 1943, a class of
240 accelerated seniors and more than twice that number
of anxious parents and relatives gathered in University
Chapel for our graduation ceremony. John Boyd, however,
was not with us. Like many students in those restless days,
John had chosen not to wait for graduation. As the oldest
son in a family with strong military traditions he wanted
nothing more than to join the Navy as soon as possible.
Accordingly, he had gone to the nearest Navy recruiting
station and enlisted.

Less than a year later, in November 1942, John's ship,
the destroyer U.S.S. *Barton,* was in the van of a task group
steaming toward a major Japanese battle force seeking to
reinforce the Japanese positions on the western end of
Guadalcanal in the Solomon Islands. During a wild night
battle in confined waters, the *Barton* took two torpedo
hits amidships, one of which almost certainly ignited her
magazines. She sank in a matter of seconds. John, a stern

gunner, was one of the few men who was able to swim off. After a night in the water the survivors were picked up by a friendly cruiser and taken to the Marine Hospital on the island of Tulaghi. John walked ashore unassisted, complaining only of constant fatigue. But on the third day doctors making their morning rounds found that Seaman 1st Class John Boyd had died during the night. Internal injuries from underwater concussions, which typically cause little or no pain and show no outward signs, were judged the cause of his death.

In February 1961, or almost 20 years after John Boyd and I first journeyed to Utah, a mounted skeleton of the carnivore *Antrodemus* was unveiled in Princeton's Museum of Natural History in Guyot Hall. Measuring 40 feet from its jaw to the tip of its long counterbalancing tail, the mount occupied most of the museum's central hall. Its preparators wisely chose to portray *Antrodemus* in an alert pose with hind legs spread apart as though about to break into a fast run and its small forefeet poised for grasping. Most noticeable, however, was *Antrodemus*'s large head. Turned to one side, it seemed to be looking at its next possible victim with a slack-jawed and leering grin that exposed all of its sharp and inwardly curving teeth.

At the time, the *Princeton Alumni Weekly* proudly noted that the *Antrodemus* mount was certainly not a case of "three bones and twenty barrels of plaster," as Mark

Twain is said to have remarked after his first view of a museum dinosaur. Indeed, there was no need for imaginative reconstruction of *Antrodemus*'s missing skeletal parts, as is often the case with dinosaur exhibits. Instead Princeton's *Antrodemus* was "all bone except for [parts of] its plastic skull."

What is more important, however, is the fact that worldwide recognition has come to the Utah quarry site in the years that followed. Although Princeton no longer participated in the excavations after the war, the work at the Cleveland quarry was continued by the University of Utah under the able guidance of Lee Stokes, along with occasional support from other universities and museums. In the process, however, there occurred one unfortunate event. *Antrodemus,* which derives from the Greek for "cave spirit" or "cave demon," was synonimized to *Allosaurus,* Greek for "other lizard." This occurred in the late 1960s when certain paleontologists claimed that *Antrodemus* was one and the same as *Allosaurus,* a dinosaur Yale professor Othniel Charles Marsh had described and named on the basis of a few skull parts and three tail vertebrae found in Colorado in the 1890s. Thus one of the most fanciful names in dinosaur taxonomy has been changed to one of the dullest. *Allosaurus* now stands in bleak contrast to the well-named *Tyrannosaurus,* "tyrant lizard"; *Brontosaurus,* "thunder lizard"; or the plate-backed Stegosaurus, "covered" or "roofed lizard." One may only suppose that Professor Marsh, who first described and named a number of dinosaurs in the 19th century, simply grew weary of the naming game. In any case the change was never challenged in the high court of taxonomy, or the International Code of Zoological Nomenclature, as sometimes happens. Thus "other lizard" it remains.

For the rest, the history of *Allosaurus* and the Cleveland quarry site reads like a litany of superlatives. What Lee Stokes first described as a "large deposit of well-preserved dinosaur bones heretofore undescribed" has proven to be a spectacular trap that has yielded a great many bones from a relatively small area. From it have come more than enough specimens to make *Allosaurus* the most completely known of all dinosaurs, which is to say that all of its bones have been found, measured, and identified. All 296 of them in its body, that is, plus 64 more in its skull. Not only that, *Allosaurus* provides the best known record of dinosaur growth stages, thanks largely to what was once known as the University of Utah's "bone barn." The barn, actually an old World War II Army barracks, housed representative parts from some 50 *Allosaurus* specimens from the Cleveland quarry collected and assembled by the University's James H. Madsen, Jr. Since these specimens represented every stage of growth—juvenile, adult, and aged—the bone barn became something of a mecca for a generation of visiting specialists to whom it is an "astounding treasure house where every detail of [allosaurian] . . . biomechanics stands revealed."

This is especially true of paleontologists most interested in predator species, since *Allosaurus*, the reigning carnivore of the late Jurassic period, is now thought by many to be the ecological counterpart of the Cretaceous-period *Tyrannosaurus*, one of the largest, fastest running, and most powerfully muscled of all flesh-eating dinosaurs.

And although *Allosaurus* constitutes almost three-quarters of its fossil fauna, the quarry has also produced some interesting herbivores. There is, for example, the rare *Camarasaurus*, a giant brontosaur known elsewhere from two localities, one in Wyoming and the other in Alberta, Canada. The rarer or less common *Barosaurus* is also represented, albeit in fragmented remains.

Still, it is in the realm of flesh-eaters that the Cleveland quarry will always be best known. In addition to *Allosaurus* it has yielded up the rare *Ceratosaurus*, a horn-skulled carnivore previously known only from parts of a single skeleton, and what has proved to be two new genera of very small carnivores. One, *Marshosaurus*, honors Yale's Othniel Charles Marsh; the other, *Stokesosaurus*, justly celebrates Lee Stokes's contributions to vertebrate paleontology.

Adding it all up, the various documented excavations at the Cleveland site have unearthed approximately 10,000 bones from which nine different animal species have been identified. Such a bounty has meant that the quarry has provided more specimens for public exhibition than any other dinosaur locality the world over. At present writing, over 50 institutions ranging from the Buffalo Museum of Science and the Los Angeles County Museum to the National Science Museum in Tokyo and the Muséum National d'Histoire Naturelle in Paris have exhibited dinosaurs from the quarry. Happily, so also has the nearby College of Eastern Utah Prehistoric Museum in Price, Utah, which in recent years has become a major repository of the Cleveland fauna.

Small wonder, then, that the quarry was designated a U.S. Natural Landmark by the Department of the Interior's Bureau of Land Management in 1966. Two years later, moreover, a small visitors center was inaugurated at the site, renamed the Cleveland-Lloyd Dinosaur Quarry to honor both the locale and Malcolm Lloyd, the Philadelphia lawyer and philanthropist who made the first excavations possible.

Some 20 to 30 people a day now visit the Cleveland-Lloyd Quarry during the summer months. To do so they must journey eight miles from the village of Cleveland over a dirt road that is impassible after thunder showers or heavy rain. Once there they may seek shelter from the heat in the attractive Visitors Center, built of native fieldstone, which in effect is a small museum. At the reception desk visitors are given a pamphlet entitled:

Meet "Al" the Allosaurus
at the
Cleveland-Lloyd Dinosaur Quarry

National Natural Landmark
Welcome

Cleveland-Lloyd Dinosaur Quarry is one of
the world's foremost dinosaur sources.
More than 30 complete skeletons,
10,000 individual bones, and several dinosaur eggs
have come from this prolific fossil bed.

Dominating the exhibit space, as well it should, is a
standing mount of *Allosaurus*. Nearby are wall mounts of
the heads and necks of *Camarasaurus*, *Barosaurus*, and
Stegosaurus. A mural depicting the ancient lakeshore where
these and other dinosaurs may have been mired and an ide-
alized dinosaur family tree round out the exhibits. Except,
that is, for the center's prized possession: one of the
dinosaur eggs first found at the site in 1987. The label
explains that it is probably one of the oldest such eggs
known and that a CAT scan has revealed a tadpole-like
shape inside, which may be an embryo. The label also
explains that the egg has multiple layers of shell, which may
indicate that the dinosaur who laid it was suffering from
severe stress. From constant predator attacks, one is
tempted to say, or struggles with muddy lake bottoms.

At present writing, excavations at Cleveland-Lloyd have
been suspended. This is not to say, however, that the
Morrison formation at the site has no more fossils. Rather,
while conducting core drillings, the Bureau of Land
Management found that the fossil-bearing Morrison

deposit continues at greater depths in the direction of and under the mesa. Thus further excavations would be a costly and difficult proposition, presenting a major problem in overburden removal, so to speak.

But visitors may still get an idea of how dinosaur fossils are found in the field by a Bureau exhibit. Although the original quarry was bulldozed over some years ago, the Bureau has built a protective metal shed over a more recent excavation pit above which is a catwalk for visitors. An ingenious label system allows the viewer to identify the different bones *in situ* in the pit and also on a schematic diagram of a dinosaur that hangs overhead.

My wife and I visited the Cleveland-Lloyd Quarry in the summer of 1993, or more than 50 years after I had first been at the site as part of the Princeton group. We toured the Visitors Center and then spent some time in the heat of the catwalk shed gazing down at the fossil bones below us. I then set out to find the sheltering boulder where John Boyd and I first pitched our tent, while my wife, who dislikes hot weather, rested in our air-conditioned rental car. At first I had some trouble in finding the right boulder. There seemed to be many more than 50 years ago, most noticeably a huge boulder twice the size of all the others that had obviously fallen down from the sandstone ridge on the top of the mesa. But soon I saw it—the overhanging, balancing rock we had called our home. It had not budged one inch and was still firmly grounded, just as John Boyd said it would be.

I sat down in the rock's shade and took a long look at the slope of the mesa in front of me. The afternoon sun beat down as hotly as ever. The tumbled rockslide of the mesa presented as harsh and as glaring a landscape as before. But for me the whole brought on a wealth of sweet-sad memories, memories of that joyful and carefree summer just before the war. I wanted to stay there, to be left there with my thoughts until the sun sank lower and the desert rocks took on more pleasing colors from the late afternoon's slanting light. But soon my wife was blowing the horn of our car, beckoning me to be on our way.

On the journey back east I kept thinking about all the distinctions that have come to the Cleveland-Lloyd Dinosaur Quarry and the good work the University of Utah has done to unearth, study, and interpret its fossil bounty. By contrast Princeton University seemed to have played a very small part, now largely forgotten. Not only did Princeton not participate in the post-war excavations, the University also did not collect any other dinosaurs and has gradually de-emphasized paleontology in general. In fact, almost a thousand bones from its Cleveland-Lloyd collections were returned to Utah in 1964—more specifically to the University of Utah—to round out Utah's collections. Then, too, following Glenn Jepsen's death in 1974, no true successor has ever filled his chair, and the recently renamed Department of Geology and Geophysical Sciences no longer supports vertebrate paleontology. Ultimately, in February 1985, the department gave most of the vertebrate fossils in the Geology Museum to Yale University and, shortly thereafter, most of the invertebrates to the Smithsonian Institution, in order to have more space for offices and library bookcases. So it has happened that the museum's most valuable specimens, ranging from the spectacular *Megatherium*, or giant sloth of Patagonia, to the finely preserved plants and insects of the Florissant shale of Colorado, have gone either to New Haven or Washington. Practically speaking, the Princeton Geology Museum has been reduced to a few small teaching exhibits that are hard to find.

Except, that is, for *Antrodemus*, the "cave demon," also known as *Allosaurus*. The standing mount, so long in preparation, is still a commanding presence in Guyot Hall, rising well above the offices and library cases. I like best to visit there on Saturday afternoons during the football season, when I am sure to be alone and an uncharacteristic quiet pervades all of Guyot. There is *Antrodemus*, all 40 feet of him, with legs spread apart as though about to break into a fast run and small forefeet held at the ready. And there is his big head, with its leering and toothy grin, still turned to one side as if looking for its next possible victim.

It is at these moments that I wish most that John Boyd were with me. I can see him looking over our dinosaur with rapt attention, noting every detail. "I'll be hornswoggled, Shorty," he would then say, "if that ain't a purty sight."

"Reckon so, Slim, reckon so," I would be expected to reply.

We might then head off together, looking for new sites to conquer. Or, perhaps, a fast game of blackjack.

THE NIGHT
OF THE WHALES
~

One January night almost 50 years ago I found myself looking straight into the eye of a large black whale. It had just finished swimming through a dense bed of kelp on its back, exposing a gleaming white underbelly. The whale's swimming motion was slow, sinuous, and obviously sensual, as though enjoying a deeply satisfying back rub. Now it had righted itself and was swimming closer into the kelp bed, the inner edge of which was not more than ten yards from the rocky beach where I stood. There it stopped for what seemed like a very long time.

Soon I became acutely aware that the whale's small beady eye was fixed on me in what looked like a malevolent glare. Yielding to a small-boy impulse, I threw a rock at the whale.

The rock hit the whale squarely on its shiny wet-black back, just behind its high dorsal fin. Instantly the whale raised its tail, brought the flukes down hard on the water, and drenched me in spray. I scrambled up the rocky beach, quite scared.

I knew the whale was a killer. "Bad feesh," said Don Clemente, my Yaghan Indian host, when the whales first came into the small cove of Harberton on Tierra del Fuego's Beagle Channel. And had I not read how killer whales had lunged up on ice floes to snatch the sleeping sled dogs of Antarctic explorers? There was reason enough to give these creatures a wide berth. It is true of course that in recent years the orca, as the killer whale is also now popularly known, has been petted, caressed, and cheered by crowds as it performs all manner of acrobatics at various aquaria, not to mention a starring role in recent feature films. There are now even orca dolls for sale. I'm told they are a very popular item at San Diego's SeaWorld. But all of this, or *Orcinus orca*'s kindly disposition toward humans, was quite unknown back in the 1940s when I was in Harberton. What was known then was that given certain conditions, killer whales might savagely attack penguins, seals, larger whales, and many other convenient forms of prey. They still do.

Even less known then was the concept of play among animals. Ethology, or the scientific study of animal behavior, was still in its infancy, concentrating mainly on mating rituals and territoriality. The idea that anyone other than ourselves might enjoy play for play's sake was not yet getting much serious attention. Certainly not in relation to the order Cetacea, at least, which includes all whales and dolphins. But that is precisely what I was privileged to observe on that January night.

What took me to Harberton in the first place was an irrational urge to reach the southern limits of the Western Hemisphere. To be more precise I wanted to explore *la tierra mas austral del mundo*, as Chileans and Argentines like to say of the Cape Horn region. I would do this entirely on my own, using only public transport wherever such existed. Along the way I had the good fortune to meet the Bridges family of Viamonte on the Atlantic coast of Tierra del Fuego, descendants of the first English missionary to have dwelled successfully among the Yaghan Indians. The Bridges kindly arranged for me to travel south across the Darwin Range, guided by two of their ranch hands, to the family's original mission station in Harberton at the eastern end of the Beagle Channel. There, I was told, various small craft might stop en route down the channel to Ushuaia, a small town with a large prison then known as the "Devil's Island of Argentina." Once in Ushuaia I could take my chances for transport to Cape Horn.

The journey across the Darwin Range, ordinarily one long day's ride, proved more difficult than usual. There were fast-flowing mountain streams to ford and bogs carpeted with brilliant yellow- and orange-colored mosses into which the horses sometimes sank to their bellies, to say nothing of snow-covered mountain passes. After a cold night on the trail—New Year's Eve, as it happened—I reached Harberton in the afternoon of the next day. There I thought my journey might come to an end, as day after day of the new year passed by with not so much as a row-boat in sight.

I spent that time exploring Harberton's rocky shores, occasionally spotting a wary fur seal or flushing nesting pairs of Magellanic flightless steamer ducks. The latter are large birds, about the size of geese, known in Spanish as *patos vapores*. They never succeed in becoming airborne, but move about quite rapidly over the surface of the water by furiously beating their small wings and churning their webbed feet, "mak[ing] such a noise and splashing," as Charles Darwin once noted, "that the effect is most curi-ous." The fur seals, much hunted in an earlier age, generally kept their distance or were quick to slither down into the protective masses of kelp. Sometimes, too, I scaled rocky headlands to view the countryside. To the north were the peaks of the Darwin Range, dusted with summer snows. To the south across the Beagle Channel was the Chilean island of Navarino, dominated by a long and low massif designated on most maps as Mount Misery. To the south-west, where the Beagle widened out to the sea, was unin-habited Picton Island, one of three small islands over which

Chile and Argentina have long quarreled and flexed their military muscle. Beyond Picton and its two neighbors lay only the great southern oceans and Antarctica.

It was about nine o'clock on a sunny evening during my second week, as I remember it, that the whales came to Harberton. They first announced their presence with a dull booming sound not unlike a distant or muffled cannon shot. I ran out of the kitchen where the camp crew was having a late supper to see three killer whales at the exact center of Harberton's small harbor. One after another the whales raised their tails, formed the flukes into cuplike shapes, and then slammed them down hard on the water surface. The result was a deep-toned and satisfying thud, loud enough to reverberate around Harberton's hills. (Humans can at least approximate the effect in a bathtub by cupping both hands and bringing them down sharply to make little depth-charge splashes.) My first thought was that the whales were trying to stun schools of small fish. I ran to get my binoculars for a closer look. But all I could see was mirror-smooth water, untracked by any fleeing fish. Gradually and almost inevitably, the thought that the whales were simply having a good time crossed my mind. There could be no other explanation.

Since the small inner harbor had a narrow inlet at its mouth not more than half a mile from where I stood, I set out half-running and half-stumbling over the rocky terrain to reach it before the whales might choose to leave. Along the way I all but tripped over a pair of the *patos vapores*, which immediately took to the water and sputtered off, squawking loudly in protest. But well before reaching the inlet, I was stopped in my tracks by a spectacular explosion. A large whale shot up out of the water, rolled over in midair, and came down with a resounding splash less than 20 yards from the shore.

Killer whales are not large as whales go, but a healthy male adult will measure more than 25 feet in length and weigh as much as six tons. To see a creature of these dimensions erupt in quiet and confined waters—in a pond, in effect—is a nerve-shattering and awesome experience. What is more, the one leaping whale was quickly joined by about four or five others, including two juveniles. Some whales cleared the water entirely, landing as loudly as possible on their backs, sides, or bellies. Others shot up for only half or two-thirds of their body length and then let themselves fall back in whatever posture gravity dictated. All joined in, adults and juveniles alike, in what I imagined could only be a joyous celebration of their chance discovery of a sheltered and secluded playground.

While this activity continued, one of the adults came into the kelp, rolled over, and began the slow and sensual swim I have previously described. This gave me a close view of one of nature's most startling black-and-white designs— the jet-black of the whale's topsides against the gleaming white of its underparts. Whale identification guidebooks generally describe the killer as having "back, sides, tail, fin and flippers black; chin, throat, chest and abdomen white." But the reader may gain a clearer picture of the contrast by imagining the white underside as flowing outward in gracefully scalloped curves from the whale's narrow tail and sweeping forward to a point at its lower jaw. All the rest is black. Except, that is, for an oval-shaped patch of white immediately above the eye and a grayish saddle immediately behind the dorsal fin present on most whales. The function of these patches, or for that matter the entire black-and-white design, is not fully understood. It may be that they help killer whales to recognize each other at a distance, since there are slight variations in the shape of the patches, not to mention the overall designs.

In time, after getting sprayed as a result of my rock throw, I happened to look back from the higher ground at the small group of whales that had first appeared at the center of the harbor. Three whales were still there, but one of the steamer ducks was missing. Then came one of those rare events that leave us with a large measure of disbelief—disbelief, as the popular expression has it, of what is happening right in front of our eyes.

At first the whales took turns coming up under the remaining duck like surfacing submarines, thus causing the poor creature to slide down their broad backs in various ungainly postures. Then one whale tired of this activity and swam close alongside the duck, curving its body to look backward as it passed. It then raised its tail and brought it down sharply. The steamer duck, now quite exhausted from repeated attempts to flee the whale's attentions, made a desperate lunge to escape the blow. But the whale's flukes did not strike the duck—indeed I do not think such was the whale's intention—instead they came down just close enough to create a great lateral thrust of water that sent the bird skidding across the surface directly to another whale. Much to my amazement the second whale promptly raised its tail and in the same manner sent the duck skidding to the third. The third passed it back to the first. So it went. Each time the weary *pato vapor* made one more feeble attempt to escape and each time the whales sent it skidding in what resembled nothing so much as an ice hockey game featuring deadly-accurate slap shots. But very soon something distracted my attention—a particularly loud splash, I think—from one of the whales nearest to me. When I looked back at the hockey players, the steamer duck was gone. I like to think that perhaps the whales had suddenly tired of their game and thus allowed the poor duck one last chance to reach the safety of the shoreline. But such a scenario, all things considered, seems unlikely.

All play must come to an end, of course, giving way in the animal world to the more serious business of the hunt. In the case of the whales who came into Harberton, the moment came very abruptly. It was as if a leader in the group had given a sharp command to leave, since all the whales swam through the harbor mouth within a very short time. Their large dorsal fins, cutting through the water like tall black sails, passed by me in what seemed a continuous review. I watched them for a long time in the waning sunlight of the summer evening as they headed out to sea toward Picton Island and the great southern oceans surrounding Antarctica. So, too, did a nervous fur seal hugging the shore quite close to me.

A week later a small schooner took me down the Beagle Channel to Ushuaia. There I found that the prison, the notorious Argentine Devil's Island, was no longer the town's principal reason for being. Rather, an airfield, some oil storage tanks, and various improved port facilities were rapidly being built to be used as a base for Argentina's Antarctic pretensions. In fact Ushuaia had been declared a *recinto militar*, or a restricted area under military governance. What's more, as luck would have it, the first Argentine Antarctic expeditionary ship was expected later in the same day of my arrival. These circumstances caused me yet another enforced stay. Not to explore ways of getting to Cape Horn, that is, but rather in getting out of Ushuaia, where I was immediately thought to be a spy. But that is another story. More important to this narrative is the fact that a month later I was in New York and eager to pass on my observations of killer whale behavior to any interested authorities.

My first stop (and only one, for reasons that will soon become clear) was the American Museum of Natural History, an institution that had been one of my favorite boyhood refuges. After various inquiries and calls from one office to another, I was eventually received by a scientist whom I supposed to be a whale expert. Patiently I read my field notes to him, pausing briefly for questions or exclamations of wonderment. But none ever came from my listener, whose face remained fixed in a patronizing smile. As clearly as any words, his silence told me he was not about to believe the unlikely observations of the young man sitting in front of him. Finished, I asked if he would like a copy of my notes. No, thank you, he replied, there was really no need, since he could scarcely forget my vivid account of such extraordinary doings.

It was, as we say today, the ultimate put-down. I left the museum feeling both humiliated and angry, certain that I would make no further attempts to reach the scientific community. Looking back, I now know that it was futile to have made the attempt in the first place. At the time, in the late 1940s, the Smithsonian Institution alone had a true whale expert, which is to say a full-time curator of whales and other marine mammals in the person of the late Remington Kellog. What is more, the study of whales there and later at the American Museum and other kindred institutions was for many years confined largely to systematics, as biologists now like to say of taxonomy, or the patient business of identifying all living things and putting them in properly classified order.

All this has changed. Whale behavior is now eagerly studied by scientists and legions of dedicated whale watchers. Although there remains very much to learn of whale life cycles, we now know more about both the play and the communication signals of a number of species, *Orcinus orca* among them. The slamming of cupped flukes on the surface of the water, which I first saw at Harberton, is now known as tail lobbing and recognized as a playful activity shared by a number of other species. The same can be said of breaching, or jumping clear of the water. This, too, is recognized as a form of play, in which killer whales and humpbacks are the absolute aerial champions. Jumping for joy, I prefer to call it, since there seems to be no other satisfactory explanation for their spectacular leaps, although some scientists prefer to think of them as "an emphatic form of audio-visual communication." After observing killers in other places, notably British Columbia, and humpbacks in Newfoundland and southeast Alaska, I have come to the conclusion that leaping most often occurs close to shore in relatively sheltered waters with plentiful supplies of small food fish or other prey. A quiet spot for leisurely dining in other words, which is reason enough for rejoicing.

Nor should anyone be surprised to see killer whales lolling about in kelp beds, as I did in Harberton. As far as we know, nearly all whales seem to welcome a sense of touch. This is especially true of the killers and their closest relatives, the dolphins. (Taxonomically speaking, killer whales *are* dolphins, or members of the family Delphinidae.) Given the opportunity they are likely to investigate even a single piece of flotsam—a stray log, for example, adrift at sea—and rub up against it. Imagine, then, the attraction of coastal waters offering rocks, fine sand or pebbles, and wavy forests of kelp. Killer whales have been observed using all three, the rocks to scratch itchy or sore spots, the bottom sand or gravel for back rubbing, and, finally, the kelp as a lubricious balm, the ointment, so to speak, after a good massage. To prolong such tactile pleasures, in fact, the killers will often lift a mass of kelp and drape it over their heads and backs.

Neither is there any mystery about killer whales responding to command, as they appeared to do when I watched them leaving Harberton. To be sure they lack the eerie and sometimes melodious songs of the humpback, recently the subject of so much study. But killer whales do use a cacophonous variety of sounds—whistles, clicks, squeaks, grunts—which carry long distances and are more than enough for a repertoire of basic communications. That they do communicate, much like other dolphins, is now an established fact. Their working vocabulary, however, remains to be translated.

But there is one form of play, if indeed it can be called that, that the killer apparently shares with no other whales or dolphins. It is the deadly cat-and-mouse game, or the torment they inflict on their prey prior to consuming it. The steamer duck episode I witnessed in Harberton is but one small example of what killers may do with larger prey species. Roger Payne and his associates, who have long studied right whales in Patagonia, and Claudio Campagna of the New York Zoological Society, who studies sea lions in the same general area, have seen small pods of killers play catch with both adult and young southern sea lions, a large species weighing up to 600 pounds. The killers literally throw the sea lions around, flaying them to death with vigorous head shakes. (Some scientists believe the flaying action helps remove the sea lion's fur pelt, which the whales normally regurgitate.) Other observers in both North and South America have seen similar cat-and-mouse tactics used against penguins and seals.

More often than not, however, play is foregone in favor of a swift attack and kill. In a startling photograph that has appeared in NATIONAL GEOGRAPHIC, one of Dr. Payne's assistants captured the moment a killer whale used its tail to hurl a large sea lion some 30 feet into the air. Jen Bartlett, the photographer, has so described the event, after patiently watching a patrolling pod of approximately six killers. "Moments later the ocean erupted and the sea lion came hurtling out of the water. The other whales moved in, and it was all over in a matter of minutes, with nothing left but scraps of meat on the surface for kelp gulls to scavenge."

Given such attacks, we are left to confront the one great apparent contradiction in killer whale behavior. How is it, we may ask, that such seemingly savage carnivores appear to enjoy friendly associations with humans and take readily to training in captivity? But here, too, answers are beginning to emerge. In the first place killer whales have absolutely no fear of anything that swims in the seas—they are, after all, top of the line predators—and most are inclined to show a nonhostile curiosity toward boats, human beings, and almost anything else that is not part of their natural environment. (This curiosity noticeably increases, moreover, wherever the whales are no longer hunted or otherwise molested; conversely, it disappears quickly whenever they find themselves threatened or the objects of too much attention.) When in 1965 an entrepreneur from the Seattle Aquarium found it necessary to dive into a temporary net enclosure holding the first two killer whales ever taken for captivity, the whales, although obviously stressed, did not attack or harm him in any way. The same proved true in subsequent encounters with the next few whales bound for other aquaria.

But more interesting and certainly more significant answers to the killer whales' dichotomy of behavior are coming from those who have studied the whales in the wild most intensively. The late Michael Bigg of the Canadian Fisheries Research Board, Kenneth C. Balcomb of the Center for Whale Research at Friday Harbor in northern Puget Sound, Alexandra Morton of Raincoast Research at Simoon Sound, near the north end of Vancouver Island, and other observers now conclude that there are two basic populations of *Orcinus orca* with different social and behavioral patterns. In the first are what might be called resident communities. They are large in number—96 whales in the case of the Puget Sound community—and are made up of two- and three-generation families that bond for life. Remaining in one general area the year around, these community whales feed on salmon and other fish that are in relatively abundant supply on our Northwest coast. They have not been seen to eat seals or other larger forms of prey.

The second grouping is composed of pods of whales, much smaller in number, that are best described as transients. Constantly on the move in pods of two to ten individuals, they subsist mainly on penguins, seals, larger whales, and other warm-blooded animals. Stomach autopsies of these transients washed up on the shores of British Columbia have shown that they may also consume such assorted fare as waterfowl, deer, and even the remains of a pig. But no fish.

In addition to opportunistic hunting, the transient whales also gather at certain specific locations at certain times of year to take advantage of large concentrations of their favored prey. A good example of this phenomenon, recently the subject of a number of nature films, may be found at Punta Norte on the Valdés Peninsula of Patagonia. Here transient pods congregate every March and April, when the pups of the southern sea lion are born. Not content with what they may kill in the water, the whales crash through the surf, effectively stranding themselves, to snatch the pups on the beach. No other whales have the ability to save themselves from a stranding, but the killers are so strong and athletic that they have no trouble squirming back into the water. So important is this seasonal feast, in fact, that parent whales patiently teach the stranding technique to their young on empty practice beaches.

After almost 20 years of intensive study and observation, Kenneth Balcomb and his associates believe the two groups, the community residents and the transients, do not interbreed and have probably been genetically isolated for a very long time. More recently A. Rus Hoelzel of the National Institutes of Health has managed to carry out DNA fingerprinting of the two groups. They are indeed genetically distinct, Hoelzel has found, so much so that "you might think they came from different oceans," as he likes to put it.

Although much more study is necessary, similarly separate groups, or races, appear to exist elsewhere. In 1979-80, the giant factory whaling ship *Sovietskaya Rossiya* purposely took 906 killer whales from Antarctic waters for scientific examination. As a result Russian scientists now propose not different groups or races, but two separate species. The first, provisionally named *Orcinus glacialis,* is noticeably smaller in all dimensions than the familiar *Orcinus orca.* It also has a slightly different cranial structure and a film of diatomaceous algae covering its skin, which gives it a yellowish cast. These yellow whales, as the Russians like to call them, live in large communities of 150 to 200 individuals and subsist almost entirely on fish, which were found to comprise 98.5 percent of their stomach contents. As their name suggests, the "yellows" stay close to the edge of the circumpolar pack ice the year around. In social organization and feeding habits, they would seem to correspond most closely to the resident communities of our Northwest coast. Nearby, but more often roaming in open water, the Russian scientists found much smaller groups easily identified as the standard *Orcinus orca.* Because these whales had no trace of yellowish coloring, the Russian scientists took to calling them "whites." Much like our Northwest coast transients, the whites traveled about in small pods averaging 10 to 15 individuals, were never seen to mix with the yellows, and subsisted mainly on other warm-blooded mammals, the remains of which constituted 89.7 percent of their stomach contents. The other warm-blooded mammals in this case were principally other whales, especially the minke, smallest of the so-called great whales. But as Soviet and other commercial whalers from the bad old days of Antarctic whaling will readily attest, the Antarctic killers will attack any of their kin regardless of size. This the whalers know not only from actual sightings but also because they often found characteristic killer-whale teeth marks on the skins of all the various species they once took. Even on blue whales, in fact, largest of all living things.

Historically the first killer whales captured for aquaria from 1965 to 1976 came from the two best known resident communities in the United States and Canada, the Puget Sound–Straits of Georgia community of almost a hundred individuals and the north Vancouver Island–Johnstone Strait community of 190. Since then, owing to mounting public reaction against further captures in both the United States and Canada, all killer whales taken for captivity have come from Iceland.

What might happen if a mature whale from one of the small transient pods—one of the offshore whales, as they are sometimes called—were suddenly introduced into an established aquarium community remains a matter of speculation. Meanwhile the popularity of *Orcinus orca* as a public attraction has had phenomenal growth. The obliging killers shoot up from the water like Polaris missiles, jump through hoops, allow trainers to ride their backs, strand themselves on tank aprons, and apparently enjoy audience participation, letting spectators pet them or even brush their teeth. The whales learn simple commands in a manner of weeks and attain what trainers like to call a performance repertoire in approximately six months. Accidents and fatalities in the training process have been remarkably few—one death by drowning, in fact, and one serious injury as a result of a performance accident. Caution, however, remains the watchword. Some whales in captivity exhibit unfriendly if not downright hostile reactions to both humans and other whales and dolphins newly introduced into their environment. These reactions may take the form of bunting or ramming the new whale or habitually drenching a poolside attendant who has somehow provoked their displeasure. A quiet approach, or time enough to get acquainted, seems the rule to follow.

Little wonder, therefore, that killer whales have become the star attraction of the aquarium world. (One recent aquarium survey has shown that attendance drops off by 50 percent without their whales.) Vancouver, Vallejo, San Diego, San Antonio, Niagara Falls, Cleveland, Orlando, Miami—all these cities and more have their performing whales. Overseas they may be seen in Japan, Argentina, Hong Kong, and France's Côte d'Azur.

With the killer whales' increasing popularity has come mounting criticism of their retention in aquaria. As the largest mammals held in captivity and one of the fastest swimming of all sea creatures, they cannot of course be kept in enclosures that begin to approximate their natural habitat, as is now the practice with some zoo animals. Nevertheless they willingly participate in training exercises, form strong bonds with their trainers, remain playful, and otherwise adjust to life in captivity with seeming enthusiasm. But captive whales are often subject to viral diseases—pneumonia is the most common—against which they have no natural defense. The life span of *Orcinus orca* has been estimated at anywhere from 40 to 80 years, with females usually outliving males. But in captivity their life expectancy appears to be much shorter. Most specimens taken for capture are young—very young, or at an average age of four and a half years according to the U.S. Department of Commerce National Marine Fisheries Service, which is charged with keeping track of all marine mammal populations. Records from the same source show that the life span for the first 30 aquarium whales that have died of known diseases since the early 1970s averaged seven and a half years following their capture.

The record, however, is everywhere improving. There are now significant numbers of whales that have spent 12 or more years in aquaria, which means they have attained sexual maturity, and a few that have passed 20, which means that they have reached the hypothetical age for grandparenting. Then, too, as aquarium directors are quick to point out, the number of baby killer whales born in captivity appears to be rising. SeaWorld, which operates four aquaria in the United States, has successfully raised four calves since 1985. Five more have been born in other aquaria and marine parks during the same period. And the Vancouver Aquarium, a model of its kind, is pointing the way with a firm policy against taking any more killer whales from the wild, relying instead on births and breeding loans from other institutions.

To the critics of Greenpeace and kindred organizations, aquarium directors maintain that performing killer whales have done more than any other single aquarium species to raise public consciousness of whales and the need for their protection. It is thus no coincidence, although something of a paradox, that the first places to show killer whales, notably Seattle and Vancouver, were also the first to see strong public reaction against their further capture. To put it another way the performing whales—"the Teddy Bears and giant pandas of the marine world" as some call them—seem to have the power to evoke both instant enthusiasm and sympathy from their audiences the world over.

Science, too, has benefited from the retention of killer whales in aquaria and marine parks. The latter have offered what in effect are the first living laboratories for marine mammal research. In the pre-dawn era of cetacean research, which is to say the pre-aquaria era, even such basic data as the exact gestation period for killer whales and other dolphins was unknown. (It is 17 months for *Orcinus orca* and 11 for *Tursiops truncatus,* or the bottlenose dolphin of performance fame.) Today, thanks to these living laboratories, studies in cetacean behavior, acoustics, genetics, hematology, general physiology, and veterinary science have all made great advances. There are very few cetacean specialists, in fact, who have not profited from the visiting fellowships and general-study facilities offered by the better aquaria.

Killer whales in confinement, it would therefore appear, are here to stay. To be sure, there are now more opportunities to observe the whales in their natural habitat through whale-watching cruises and day trips. For this reason it is the view of some conservationists and humane society critics that whale watching in the wild should be the only way to see them. But if only a very small fraction of the millions of interested viewers who now flock to aquaria to see killer whales perform—over eight million annually visit the four SeaWorlds in the United States alone—were interested in taking boats to the best known killer whale concentration areas of the Seattle–Vancouver region, the result might well be disastrous. The very size of the flotilla necessary to take the public to these areas and the resulting commotion of marine traffic in such confined waters as the Johnstone and Georgia Straits might very well cause the disappearance of the north Vancouver Island and Puget Sound communities.

Still, it is hard not to sympathize with the position of both camps. For myself it has been a rewarding experience to renew acquaintance with *Orcinus orca* through the convenience of public showings. Even as I might wish these noble animals could forever roam free, I find myself thrilled by watching them display their grace and athleticism in the intimacy of an aquarium setting—to the point of joining the cheers of the crowd, I must confess, or sharing the sense of wonderment and joy of the youngest spectators. Yet these are not the occasions that remain indelibly in my mind.

Rather, it is the memory of the night the whales came to Harberton almost 50 years ago. Every incident of what was in effect a private showing in that wild and lonely amphitheater remains remarkably clear. The tail lobbing, the explosive breaches, the rolling in the kelp, the steamer duck hockey game, all these are like so many freeze-frame images that can be brought instantly and brilliantly to mind. But the image I like best, the one I think of most often, is of the whales' departure. It is the image of the tall black sails of their dorsal fins passing by in review, heading out the Beagle Channel to the great southern oceans and Antarctica in the waning light of a summer evening.

THE FISHES OF
PELELIU

~

O ne August morning many years ago in the time
of World War II, I walked carefully along a beach
in the Pacific islands of New Hebrides (now
Vanuatu). The sun was quite hot and so was the sand, to the
point that I could feel its warmth through the soles of my
aging sneakers. But I kept on walking for some distance, trying not to think about the heat.

It was a relief, therefore, when the beach gave way to a
rocky peninsula, and behind it, a quiet cove well shaded by
tall palms and casuarina trees. The water in the cove was
clear, unruffled by any breeze. Looking down into it, I could
easily make out a submarine garden with many different
corals, brightly colored anemones, and waving sea fans.
I had found what I was looking for.

84

Here was a place I could try out my Hawaiian spear-fisherman's goggles, the simplest of devices for underwater vision, made of wood, plain glass, and a strap of automobile-tire inner tube. (Rubber-mounted face masks had yet to arrive on the scene.) After fitting the strap over the back of my head, I carefully adjusted the wooden rims of the goggles so that they fit the bones around my eyes as tightly as possible. These things done, I slipped quietly into the water.

The first viewing of a healthy coral reef community all but beggars description. You are suddenly immersed in a new world where nature has shed all reserve and allows herself to be seen in her most flamboyant form. In this, my first such viewing, I crouched comfortably on a patch of sand in the quiet cove, coming up for quick gulps of air only as often as necessary. I had the feeling I was half-sitting and half-floating in the middle of a natural amphitheater. Corals of many different kinds—staghorn, fire, boulder—served as the backdrop of my theater. Fish were the players of the center stage, swimming slowly or darting quickly across its proscenium in extravagantly colored and intricately patterned costumes. I saw small bright yellow fish, always swimming in pairs, with thinly compressed bodies that might fit in the palm of your hand. They had delicate pointed mouths and their flat sides were adorned with dotted stripes in horizontal, vertical, and even crosshatched patterns. Some had black spots at the base of their tails; others had vertical stripes running above and below their eyes. I saw blue-colored fishes, most notably a small and chunky-bodied fish that seemed to have been dipped in a dark blue coloring agent that covered all of its body except for a white spot on its back and thin yellow borders on its ventral fins. I saw one slightly larger fish with a green head, yellow shoulders, and pink body. And everywhere I looked under or near coral heads there were small red-scaled fish with large eyes. They preferred to stay partially hidden or, if not, very close to the sheltering coral.

In time, as all who have used them will understand, my Hawaiian goggles began to give me a headache. Resting on shore, I took my aging paperback copy of the *Colored Guide to Pacific Fishes* out of my knapsack and tried to identify what I had seen. The guide was woefully deficient as far as precise identifications went, but at least it was useful in determining some general categories. I had seen butterflyfish, an angelfish, a species of wrasse, and some soldierfish, or the little red fish with big eyes also known as squirrelfish, to mention a few.

After another dive I could add to my list one sea snake with brightly colored silver and black bands. The fact that it was a snake and not an eel-like fish was immediately apparent by its slow and snakelike movements through the water. It was highly poisonous, the guide said, but not aggressive. I also saw some thick-bodied moray eels poking their gaping jaws out of coral tunnels. Nearby, seemingly embedded in the coral or growing out of it, were two wavy masses of fleshy matter colored deep blue and more or less in the shape of opposing lips. They were so utterly strange looking and, I thought, possibly toxic, that I refrained from touching or trying to handle them. This was a wise decision, I would later learn.

Walking home to my encampment, I looked forward to returning to what I now regarded as my private cove. Fish watching would be the ideal way to pass away my waiting time in the New Hebrides.

The next day, however, I was ordered to pack up and board one of two large troop transports in the harbor of Espiritu Santo. Two weeks later the transports were part of a larger armada of warships and other transport and supply ships standing off the island of Peleliu in the Palau archipelago in the western Pacific. While we waited, battleships and cruisers fired their big 14- and 16-inch guns at the Japanese-held islands. As they arched overhead, their shells made a sound like the tearing of silk, followed by earth-shaking thumps as they landed on Japanese positions. After about a week of thus standing offshore, the Marine air support unit of which I was part received word that the Japanese airfield on Peleliu had been secured by the First Marine Division and duly repaired. We were therefore ordered to pack our gear and prepare to go over the side of our ship to some landing craft waiting below.

So it happened that on a September morning under a

hot equatorial sun we lined up along the starboard side of the transport carrying heavy packs to which were attached rifles, tent rolls, pick axes, and sharply pointed spades with folding handles. I puzzled over why we were issued rifles, since we were all categorized as noncombatants, the more so in my case as a naval officer who had not had any rifle or combat training. But all thoughts on this subject were quickly interrupted by a shouted order to go over the side and climb down some cargo nets draped over the ship's side to the landing craft below. This was hardly an easy task, considering the wide mesh of the cargo nets and the burdens we bore.

But we all descended without mishap, and the landing craft quickly took us ashore on the east coast of Peleliu. We then made our way over a crushed-coral path that skirted some bug-infested mangrove swamps. Along the way we passed a wrecked jeep and a burned-out Japanese tank inside of which were the charred remains of its two operators. Soon we could see the outlines of what the map called Umurbrogol Mountain, a huge massif of coralline limestone honeycombed with caves, which the Japanese held and had enlarged into a complex defensive fortress. Soon rechristened Bloody Nose Ridge, it would require many lives and many months to capture. From that direction we periodically heard the heavy thud of a mortar shell, quickly followed by the crackling of rifle fire. Everywhere we went the smell of death was heavy in the air.

My work in aerial photographic intelligence at first kept me thoroughly occupied. On Peleliu it was especially necessary to keep a photographic eye, so to speak, on the nearby islands of the Palau archipelago, which in military vocabulary had to be neutralized, not conquered. About 35 miles to the north was the island of Babelthuap, largest of the Palau group, where the Japanese had tauntingly spelled out Welcome Yankee in huge letters on the bomb-pocked runway of their principal airfield. A short distance to the south was Koror Island, site of Palau's largest town and prewar commercial center. It was also home to the Japanese navy yard and a submarine base. Consequently the island fairly bristled with well-emplaced antiaircraft guns. Below Koror was a no-man's-land of spectacular jungle-covered islands that twisted and turned in serpentine patterns. They bore strange names like Urukthapel, Arakabesan, Eil Malk, and Ngeregong, and they stretched like a giant jigsaw puzzle 20 miles south almost to Peleliu.

After about a week it was possible to steal away from my work in the late afternoon, when the day's sorties had been flown and the aerial photographs quickly reviewed for surprises. On the first such occasion I quickly stuffed my goggles, the *Colored Guide,* a notebook and pencil, and my old sneakers into a small over-the-shoulder ditty bag. Thus equipped I struck out for Peleliu's southwest coast, which I knew from photographs was graced by over a mile of uninterrupted beach. Extending out all along this beach was a fringing coral reef. It was exceptionally broad, or between 200 and 300 yards wide, and it had been the scene of the First Marine Division's difficult amphibious assault. After a short walk, I was able to stand on low dunes and survey the mile-long beach. It was now a quiet and deserted place, a kind of cemetery where wrecked tanks, shell casings, and other detritus of war were the only tombstones.

But at the far end of the reef there was a line of small waves marking the end of shoal water and the beginning of the ocean deep. I imagined this was the place to find healthy corals and many more tropical fish.

I was not disappointed. The fringing reef was easy to wade, given protective footwear, since its floor was for the most part well compacted coralline rubble. But well before the reef edge I came to an area where there were patches of sand and large coral heads, each with its own small aquarium of resident and transient fish. I therefore put on my goggles and half-swam, half-waded to view them. Once again I saw beautiful angelfish, oddly colored wrasses, and some butterflyfish, usually in pairs, not to mention many others I could not identify. I particularly remember watching a larger fish, almost the size of a freshwater bass, with a surrealistic blend of blues, greens, and large pink-edged scales. It also had a blunt head and seemed always to be swimming very close to the coral, often bumping into it. In fact it looked as if it was grazing on the coral, trying to make a meal out of the live polyps. I later read in my guide, however, that the fish were instead feeding on a film of algae which grows on most coral rock, along with bits of the rock itself. The fish was a parrotfish, the guide said, so-called because its mouth was a beak made of fused teeth well suited to nibbling and crushing. In time I would see at least three species of this fish, each with its own distinctive version of the biblical coat of many colors.

Also swimming close to the coral heads or hiding within them were the fish popularly known as triggerfish. When viewed from the side their bodies take on the approximate outline of a diamond, their "triggers" being in fact the first two spines of their dorsal fins. These along with a bony knob at the base of their stomachs allow the fish to wedge and lock themselves, top to bottom, in tight coral crevices. This done, nothing can dislodge the sometimes pugnacious triggerfish (as I found to my discomfort, trying to do so with my bare hand) unless the second spine of the dorsal fin is depressed, after which the first and larger spine will unlock.

The triggerfish, too, were not without colorful and eye-catching dress. In fact one of the most exotic of all reef fish, the humuhumu of Hawaiian song, has such an array of colors in sharp and angular juxtaposition that scientists have given it the popular name of Picassofish. There are five species of Picassofish, moreover, popularly known as the blackbelly, the Arabian, the halfmoon, the humuhumu, and the wedge Picassofish. The latter, incidentally, is well named, since it wedges itself in a suitable cranny in the surge near the edge of reefs. This is water not favored by many other small reef fish, because it requires effort to hold position or forage. The wedge Picassofish, by contrast, rests locked in its cranny and waits calmly for suitable feeding opportunities. This and other triggerfish are popular additions to saltwater aquariums. But as guidebooks will mention, they are often found to be ill-tempered.

On a subsequent trip, not very far out on the reef, I found two wavy masses of fleshy matter that looked like lips, much like what I had first seen in the New Hebrides. But now they were rather small, less than a foot in length, and their color was a yellowish brown, not deep blue. This time I touched the lips with a rusty bayonet I had started to carry; the lips instantly retracted, exposing two rows of deeply serrated teeth of shell that slowly clamped shut in perfect occlusion. Could this be the celebrated giant clam of the Pacific, I began to wonder? It was certainly no giant, but something I had read in the past about the giant *Tridacna*, the great clam of legend that clasped the hands and feet of doomed pearl divers in a viselike grip, made me think of it. Perhaps this was a juvenile of the species. But how could it possibly grow? It was wedged so tightly in its coral matrix that it was difficult at first to tell where the coral stopped and the clam's shell began. It was all very puzzling.

By this time, too, I had seen such a great variety of reef fish, many of them with brilliant colors and striking patterns, that I began to wonder why this was so. Groping toward a possible answer, I remembered something I had heard in a college biology course about the ratio of numbers of species in a given area to the size of their individual populations. Going north toward the Arctic, for example, one finds fewer and fewer species. But what species there are are there in very large populations. Examples include the caribou, one of only two species of four-footed ruminants in the high Arctic, or the lemming, one of a very few rodents. Going south, however, the opposite comes into play. The closer one gets toward the equator, the more the number of species increase. But the populations of these many different species tend to be very small. Examples include the numerous plants, insects, and small mammals that live only in specialized microclimatic areas of the tropical rain forest.

The same equation exists in the sea, of course. And what did one find in the seas approaching the equator, I began to ask myself? Why, the great variety of coral reef fish I was now viewing. Certainly I never saw any schools of the various fish that kept close to the gardens of coral. Many in fact seemed always solitary, while others swarm about in pairs. Obviously, with such small numbers, fish of the same species might have problems in finding a suitable mate. There would be problems, to put it more strongly, in assuring viable populations.

Yes, that was it. I congratulated myself on being on the

brink of an important discovery. All those yellows, blues, greens, blacks, purples, all those elaborate patterns were clearly of great help to the fish in finding a breeding partner. They were the ways a male might signal, "I am over here, right on top of this brain coral," so to speak, to a nearby female. They were essential to breeding success, I supposed.

My theory was only in part correct, I would learn much later. Today scientists will tell you the striking colors and patterns are indeed an aid to species recognition. But they are of limited use, since colors under water tend to become blurred and indistinct at between six and ten feet. There is, however, a much more wondrous, a much more important aid to breeding success, which first began to be studied in the years after World War II. Briefly stated, we now know that the majority of reef fish are capable of sex change. Many of them, moreover, are hermaphrodites. The females of most wrasse and parrotfish, for example, are able to change sex into more colorful males, as necessary, there-after known as secondary or terminal males, which become dominant over others. The mere presence of such terminal dominant males will inhibit other females from doing the same. There are other highly complex hermaphroditic processes, including some where a single female will be dominant and her mere presence will inhibit young males from changing over to females. Conversely if the dominant female should be removed from a small coral-head colony, a male will change to replace her. And so on, one might say, to keep a proper balance between the sexes.

On a subsequent outing I waded and swam slightly beyond the far edge of the reef. To be at the very edge—at the drop-off of some reefs—is like experiencing a kind of personal Everest. You look down a very steep slope where massive coral boulders have broken off the reef and tumbled down, leaving valleys behind them. You look down and down, that is to say, until the slope fades away to a dark and forbidding infinity unlike any seen on land. It seems to tell you to stay away, this infinity, warning you that beyond it is only a forbidden world where light never penetrates.

Along such reef edges up near the surface, you can often find a passing parade of predators—jacks, trevally, snappers, barracuda, sharks—that habitually swim there. On this occasion I did indeed find a predator, although not in the circumstances I might have wished. Some rolling surges from a distant storm were breaking into fair-size waves on the normally calm reef. With the water here over my head, I was having problems holding ground. I decided to take one quick look underwater and then retreat closer to the shore. To my amazement a very large barracuda—a great barracuda, that is, also known as *Sphyraena barracuda*, not to be confused with six other species—was swimming very slowly around me. The fish was longer than I am tall, I am sure, or a good six feet from the tip of his bullet-shaped jaws to the end of his tail. He kept circling me, ever watchful and with what can only be described as a baleful eye. I kept my eye on him as well, with my rusty bayonet at the ready, until I realized that sooner or later I would have to start swimming toward more shallow grounds. This proved very difficult with sneakers and the bayonet, which I felt essential to retain. Surely the commotion I caused kicking and flailing would provoke an attack, I thought. But none occurred. I stopped when the water was chest high for another look. There he was, the one and only *Sphyraena barracuda*, still circling me and ever watchful. I therefore started to tread water until it was at the level of my hips. Another look and the great fish was still with me, ever circling.

I am ashamed to say that I then tread water all the way to shore without even pausing. Today's scuba divers and snorkelers will tell you that such frightened reactions are unnecessary. It is simply the barracuda's inherent curiosity, they insist, that makes it follow you so persistently. If this unnerves you, it is only necessary to push or punch it in the nose to discourage its inquisitive habits.

But such things were not generally known in the 1940s. And, lest we forget, it is still very dangerous to be in a barracuda's presence if you have even a trace of fresh blood on or near your body. This is also true if you happen to be wearing a small silvery bracelet or some other luminous object. The barracuda will then think it a small fish and you will suffer a nasty attack. After all, the barracuda is at all times a voracious predator, quicker and more efficient than sharks in snapping up smaller reef fishes.

Refreshing and sometimes exciting as these excursions might be, the war was never very far away. Less than a thousand yards from our tent encampment, or within high-power rifle range, were the ridges and pocket valleys of the southern end of Umurbrogol Mountain. Most of the valleys had steep walls 60 to 90 feet high, deep within which lay the Japanese cave defense system. In some places the cave openings high on these walls had been equipped with doors of steel armor plating, which could be opened to fire mortar or small artillery rounds and then quickly closed for concealment. It was in these places especially that the handsome gull-winged Corsairs of Marine Fighter Squadron 114 flew what have often been called the shortest missions in the history of military aviation. "We didn't even have time to retract our landing gear," the pilots said of them, meaning they took off, made a sharp turn to the north, dropped a 500-pound napalm bomb in one of the pocket valleys, and then landed to be rearmed with another such bomb to repeat the mission. The jungle-covered walls were thus burned away and a uniform chalk-white valley laid bare. At night under the glare of phosphate parachute shells the landscape took on a ghostly lunar aspect.

Sometimes, too, bullets and shell fragments buzzed

through our tent sites and workplaces like a swarm of angry hornets, as for example when a Japanese shell from Bloody Nose Ridge exploded a nearby ammunition dump. By night, suicidal or hungry Japanese soldiers sought to infiltrate our encampment, often hiding in the little underground bunkers they themselves might have previously dug.

But the fishes and corals of Peleliu were a constant and joyful escape. In time I was joined by my friends Jim Scott, a fellow Naval Reserve photo interpreter, and Bill Parfitt, who ran a mobile photo lab equipped with a refrigerator that kept film from spoiling in the tropical heat, not to mention beer and soft drink rations, which made him very popular. Parfitt liked to explore the east side of the island, which had some close-in surf, and together we shared the Hawaiian goggles and a new French rubber-mounted face mask my family had just sent me. The variety of fish here was not as great as out on the fringing reef. But it pleased me to see Bill's first reactions to the underwater world. Swimming close by, he would yank one of my arms and point with exaggerated or comic signs to a strange-looking parrotfish or a colorful butterflyfish. Coming up for air, we exchanged accounts of what we had seen with great excitement.

On other occasions we also explored the land, looking at odd trees and plants or trying to catch ugly land crabs. For such trips I took along an armed forces booklet called the *Castaways' Baedeker*. How it got into my hands I do not know, but its aim was to tell downed airmen or shipwrecked sailors how to survive on so-called desert islands, or more accurately, the small green islets that dot the atolls of the Pacific. The *Baedeker* told us not to rely on the milk of mature coconuts found on the ground as a substitute for drinking water. In time the milk would prove to be too strong a purgative, and we might physick ourselves to death. Rather we should use the slightly flavored water of the green nuts in the crown of the palms. To this end the *Baedeker* gave instructions on the use of a beltlike foot sling as an aid to climbing. (I have a photograph Parfitt took of me following instructions on a tree that had a gentle slope near its base; I am smiling and looking upward, but in truth the photograph shows the point just before I slipped and fell.) The *Castaways' Baedeker* also had splendid illustrations of the pandanus tree, also popularly known as the screw pine, and a small tree called the fish-poison vutu. The pandanus, the fruit of which is ground by some Pacific islanders into flour for making bread, was easy to identify. This was not quite the case with a tree that certainly looked to us like the fish-poison vutu, the fruit of which was said to stun small fish in tidal pools. Bill Parfitt and I therefore laboriously followed instructions and chopped up many small pieces of the nutlike fruit and broadcast them into what we thought was a suitable tide pool. To our delight small fish appeared from everywhere. To our surprise, however, the fish started to eat our offerings, sometimes rushing to capture the best bits. We waited for the vutu to have the promised effect. But it never came, despite a long wait. Undoubtedly we misidentified our vutu. But whatever it was we did use might prove a nutritious supplement for fish farming, so eagerly did our little fish consume it. Now there was an idea, we joked. We could start a fish-food business after the war.

I also continued to visit the reef edge alone, which in the words of my companions was a far piece away. There were many new fish—families and categories of fish, in fact—to discover. There were the ugly little scorpionfish that stay well camouflaged near or in the bottom rubble, which the *Colored Guide* described as having highly venomous dorsal fin spines. Or the bizarre frogfish, a fat and globular bottom-dwelling fish with upturned eyes and mouth, above which is a single spine with a fleshy tip that the fish uses as a fishing rod and lure. When a smaller fish comes to inspect the lure, the frogfish swallows it whole with lightning speed. There were also different moray eels, and once, to my great joy, I finally found two great wavy lips of fleshy matter, colored a deep indigo blue, just as I had seen them in the New Hebrides. Once again I touched them with my rusty bayonet and they instantly retracted. Then came those deeply serrated teeth, closing in a tight fit until they were hard to distinguish from the surrounding coral matrix. Now I was sure. This was truly *Tridacna gigas*, the giant clam of the Pacific, each shell of which is large enough to serve as a small child's bathtub. But how had it gotten there, well out on the reef slope? How, to be more specific, had it moved from the small juvenile form of a different color often seen closer in toward shore? The puzzle remained.

It was not until many years later that I learned from Smithsonian colleagues what I should have deduced all along. The juveniles of my imagination were simply another species of *Tridacna*. Like those of nearly all mollusks, the free-swimming larvae of the *Tridacna gigas* eventually fall to the bottom. Wherever they fall, whether on sand or in a coral crevice, there they remain to grow. They grow to a remarkable size, moreover, measuring four feet across and weighing up to 500 pounds.

Eventually the monotony of routine and the sense of time hanging heavy spread to everyone on Peleliu. By October 30, or a month and a half after D-Day, the Japanese were still not routed from the limestone caves of Umurbrogol Mountain, and the 81st Army Division had begun to replace the battle-weary First Marine Division, which had lost 1,121 killed and 5,142 wounded on Peleliu. Although the Palau campaign had been justified as a staging base and protective eastern bastion for the invasion of the Philippines, General MacArthur had irrepressibly launched his assault on Leyte ten days earlier, while the Marines were still in the heat of battle. As more than one military historian has pointed out, Peleliu was bypassed before it was conquered.

The two fighter squadrons of Marine Air Group 11 to which our support group was attached were ordered to remain. They were to continue to neutralize the other islands of the Palau group, and they were to continue to fly wide-ranging patrols over largely empty sectors of the Pacific. Simply stated, it was more of the same, though the war was moving ever farther away.

Under such circumstances, as was their custom, the military high command thought it imperative to keep their units fully occupied, to demonstrate that the war in the western Pacific was being prosecuted on all possible fronts. Some of the minicampaigns that followed were ill conceived and unnecessary; others were at least interesting or, in some cases, droll. In the latter category was one born of information gathered from Palau natives who had escaped the Japanese-held islands to our north. There was once some form of Japanese weather station or possibly a radio-listening post, the natives said, on an island called Pulo Anna, one of three tiny fly-specks on the map about 220 miles southwest of Peleliu. Based on these reports, a Corsair photo plane was sent with escorting fighters to photograph the island.

The photographs that came back from Pulo Anna showed no signs of any human population, much less a weather or radio station. But it was still possible that there could be people and buildings on the island, since its land area was covered by a dense canopy of tropical vegetation that concealed everything underneath it. In any case I thought it an attractive enough island and began imagining what it would be like to go there. Pulo Anna was oval-shaped, not more than 250 yards in its longest dimension, and it was completely encircled by a fine-looking fringing reef of pure white sand. Surely the reef would have some interesting fish, I thought, considering its isolated geographic location. I might even discover some new species unknown to science, since some coral reef fish were said to be of very limited distribution. Yes, all things considered, Pulo Anna might be a good place to be marooned. With a *Castaways' Baedeker*, I might even try living off the land and the sea in blissful solitude.

The second event in the Pulo Anna campaign, if indeed we may call it that, was the high command's order to send another photo plane, this time a P-38 Lightning with nose cameras, for angled shots. I asked the pilot to fly low along the reefs of the island's long dimensions. Perhaps a low-angle shot might reveal buildings or dwellings just under the trees at the back of the beaches.

The photographs from this sortie revealed an unexpected sequence I will never forget. First came a shot of a native completing his morning toilet near the reef's outer edge, not an uncommon practice on the Pacific islands, where it is said natives can synchronize their bowel movements to coincide with high tides. In the next shot the native had almost reached the beach. In the third he had reached it and was running hard. The fourth and final shot showed him disappearing into the bush.

It was my job as always to report this finding in proper militarese. I did so as required, through various channels, and with copies for everyone from the Com Gen of the 81st Army Division to CincPac-CincPoa, or the Commander in Chief of the Pacific Ocean Area. The substance of my report as I remember it ran as follows:

> SUBJECT: Pulo Anna Island, Caroline Islands, Western Pacific Lat. 4°40'N Long. 131°58'E
>
> SUMMARY: Subject island is inhabited. Annotated Photo A shows individual seated in water in NE segment fringing coral reef. Photo B shows subject individual at water's edge, commencing to cross beach. Photos C and D reveal same individual successfully transiting beach and diving into forest cover. No meteorological installations, no buildings, no dwelling observed. No other signs human habitation observed.

In spite of my downbeat assessment, the Commander of the Western Caroline Area ordered the 81st Infantry Division to make further studies of the island, with an eye to its future occupation. If indeed Pulo Anna was not held by the Japanese, the thought was that it would be a good site for a long-range navigation station, better known as Loran. Such a station on Pulo Anna, along with others to the north in the Mariana Islands, would give good coverage of the 600 miles of open ocean west to the Philippines.

After more aerial sorties revealed there were few Japanese troops on three other tiny islands nearby, the high command ordered a reconnoitering party to land on Pulo Anna to gather more intelligence on Japanese forces in the area and to select a site for a possible Loran station. Accordingly, a landing party of 35 officers and men, including infantry, engineers, and four natives familiar with Pulo Anna, made an overnight voyage to the island aboard two LSI's (Landing Ship Infantry). Much as I tried, I could not get permission to accompany them. The best that I could do was make the Japanese language interpreter, an officer from our support unit who was judged essential to the operation, promise to bring back a full account of all that transpired. He agreed to do this.

The interpreter was as good as his word. Shortly after his return he told me the members of the landing force reached Pulo Anna by night, as planned, and then waded ashore after the first light of dawn. They next moved cautiously inland with infantrymen in the lead, rifles at the ready. Not far from the island's southern shore they found a cluster of four or five native dwellings with pandanus and palm-thatched roofs. Inside them a few natives could be seen peeking through doorways or the cracks in their huts. They were obviously nervous. Some smiled thinly, but none elected to come out in the open.

The colonel in charge, who had obviously seen too many Tarzan movies, started patting his chest and saying, "We friends, we friends." At the same time he shook some bags of candy he had brought for just such an occasion, indicating through body language he would give them these and many more.

After what the interpreter called a long and embarrassing interlude, an old man, thin and with bad teeth, came out of his hut and bowed with respect. Soon four or five other natives came out and stood close by him. The colonel then asked the interpreter to tell them we were friendly Americans, after which he should inquire about the Japanese weather station.

"I am Uruk," the old man answered. "I am Uruk, born to the clan of the sun god Lukunor. Lukunor took as his wife Felta, she of the island called Merir. Felta was born of the great chief Rugog and his wife Ngerchelong. The sun god Lukunor and Felta had as issue a princely boy known as Rumung of Yap—"

"Ask him about the Japanese weather station," the colonel interrupted.

"I am Uruk, of the clan of the sun god Lukunor," the old man answered again. "Lukunor took as his wife Felta, she of the islan—"[1]

Again the colonel interrupted and the same exchange began again, until the interpreter felt constrained to tell the colonel that genealogy is very important to Pacific islanders

---

[1] The dialogue is a reconstruction of what the interpreter told me, using randomly selected Micronesian place and clan names.

and especially so to the Micronesians of the Caroline Islands. It would therefore be more productive to let the old man complete his line of descent, which to him and many other natives is like a calling card. Then he could inquire about the Japanese.

This strategy was agreed upon. The old man then proceeded to trace his descent through several generations, at times doing so in a rhythmic chant. In the end he said that the honored visitors should understand that he and his family—they were six altogether—were of the highest caste, of the royal line. He in fact was the paramount chief of Pulo Anna, while the other five persons on the island—its total population was 11—were commoners. This established, the chief asked what was it the honored visitors wanted to know, since he had forgotten the question.

My friend the interpreter bowed politely, to show due respect to the paramount chief, and asked him again about the Japanese weather station. Or, was it possibly a radio-listening post? The old man said in response that, yes, he remembered the Japanese, but that was many moons past, or at least four or five years ago. Pulo Anna had received no more visitors since then, he added.

After a thorough survey which suggested Pulo Anna would be a suitable location for a Loran site, the colonel ordered the expeditionary force to return to Peleliu. A little more than three weeks later the Pulo Anna occupation force, as it was known, made its way to the island on an LST

(Landing Ship Tank). Under the command of a brigadier general, the force consisted of detachments from an infantry division, three engineer batallions, one medical batallion, some signal corps units, and an amphibian truck company. Within one week, or on December 1, 1944, the families of the paramount chief and the five commoners witnessed what was surely a high point in the history of Pulo Anna, or the christening of an operational Loran system.

In the weeks and months that followed, through the Christmas and New Year holidays, I continued my underwater explorations. I also tried to think of ways to promote a trip to Pulo Anna. Although I knew something about navigation and nautical charts, I could hardly pose as an expert on the recent advances in Loran. Perhaps an aid mission to Pulo Anna would sound better. After all an island with a total population of 11 was marginal. Given an epidemic of flu or a severe typhoon, it might be eliminated and the royal line of the sun god Lukunor would come to an end.

But these and all other ideas about how to make life on Peleliu more interesting suddenly faded to insignificance. One day in February, I received orders stating that I would be eligible in one month for an R & R, or a rest and recuperation leave, in Australia, This, of course, seemed the happiest event of my military career. What better place to continue my pioneer skin diving than the Great Barrier Reef. And everyone said the young ladies of Australia were attractive and very friendly. I was beside myself with joy.

But as is sometimes said in the military, orders cannot be considered final until they are executed. Two weeks later my R & R was amended and I was ordered to proceed to an aircraft carrier as soon as possible.

Three weeks later I was aboard the U.S.S. *San Jacinto*, at the height of the Okinawa naval campaign, to which the Japanese responded with their celebrated kamikaze air attacks.

Nearly a lifetime has passed since the events I have described. Palau is now a fast-growing commercial and tourist center of the western Pacific. Scuba divers and snorkelers arrive there in prearranged tours; they stay in semiluxurious hotels on Koror and are speeded by motor launch to the maze of serpentine islands to the south. Cruise ships regularly include the Palau archipelago on their itineraries.

In the past the giant *Tridacna* clam used to be left alone by native islanders and only chopped out of the coral as an emergency food supply. Now the clams are sold for food and are very popular with landscape architects, who use their shells as fountain basins in garden statuary. Scuba divers uproot them for souvenirs. Palau has become a center for this trade to the point that *Tridacna* has received protected status there and in nearby islands. But enforcement is said to be lax.

No tourists go to Peleliu, nor do many veterans of the

costly battles of Umurbrogol Mountain. My friend Otis Carney, a marine pilot who was with me on Peleliu, made a return visit there not long ago. He found all the traces of war completely hidden. Lush tropical vegetation has now reconquered the island, covering airfield runways, buildings, and even all the pocket valleys and heights of Umurbrogol. The Marine cemetery has been discontinued; the last bodies of those killed were exhumed in 1952 and sent to the States for reburial.

Some few Japanese have long come to Peleliu to visit a Shinto shrine near the southern end of Umurbrogol Mountain to honor their forebears who died in their defense of the island. Not until 1984 did former Marines, mainly a First Division colonel and a master sergeant, succeed in establishing a monument honoring the American dead. It is a small stone of red granite. Its inscription reads:

IN MEMORY OF THE MARINES
WHO GAVE THEIR LIVES IN THE SEIZURE
OF PELELIU AND NGESEBUS ISLAND
FROM THE JAPANESE DURING THE
PERIOD 15TH SEPTEMBER THROUGH
15TH OCTOBER 1944

I think back about Peleliu with some frequency. There are some things that I would prefer never to have seen, some costly and ill-conceived campaigns that should never have been mounted. But there is one memory I always

treasure. It is, of course, the fringing reef and its spectacular array of fish and corals. In many ways it has been a gift,
since I continue to view the underwater world of the tropics, notably in Belize and the Bahamas, with the same
excited curiosity as the first time I strapped on my
Hawaiian goggles in the New Hebrides. There are few
greater pleasures in the natural world than gliding along
wearing a modern face mask, snorkel, and swim fins, viewing one magic coral castle after another and the fish that
inhabit them. It remains a resource, a refreshing and
renewing experience, much as it was on Peleliu. What is
more, there are now reasonably comprehensive colored
guides to tropical reef fish, with some giving descriptions
and color illustrations for almost 2,000 species.

It has long been my wish to return to Peleliu, and I mean
soon to do it. I would not tarry long in Koror or other of
the northern islands. I would make right for the outer edge
of the fringing reef, never mind the barracudas or the long
spines of the black sea urchins that once gave me an infec-
tion in my right foot.

And, of course, I would certainly try once again to
get to Pulo Anna. By happy coincidence I have a neighborhood friend, Ralph Rack, who formerly served as
Pharmaceutical Consultant to the Federated States of
Micronesia, based in Pohnpei. Ralph has brought me the
news that Pulo Anna is still inhabited, although the population is very low. He tells me that the reason many tiny

islands in the Carolines remain inhabited is because land is the most treasured possession of all Micronesians. The land that is theirs is the land of their ancestors, whose lines they must perpetuate. Thus they tend to remain, even on the smallest islands. In Ralph's time, or up until 1992, a dispensary and supply ship sent from Koror visited Pulo Anna four times a year, but now it comes but twice a year.

I continue to dream about going there. Pulo Anna is an oval-shaped island, little more than a mile long, completely encircled by a fine-looking fringing reef of pure white sand. Surely the reef would have some interesting fish, perhaps some species of limited distribution unknown to science. As a matter of fact, Pulo Anna might be the ideal place to be marooned with a *Castaways' Baedeker,* to live off the land and the sea . . .

Or have I said all this before?

THE RIVER
AND THE HOWLERS
~

There is a genus of monkeys native to both Central and South America to which the 18th-century French statesman and taxonomist Count Étienne de la Ville Lacépède gave the name *Alouatte*, which sounds very much like the French word for skylark. No one, scientists included, can say why. Be that as it may, *Alouatta*, as it is now spelled, has another and much more important distinction. It is the only monkey that cannot normally be kept in zoos. Some zoo directors have tried, but *Alouatta* requires a highly specialized diet of tropical fruits and leaves. More than that, its presence in zoo monkey houses eventually makes life intolerable for all the other simians, to say nothing of humans living anywhere nearby. This is undoubtedly because *Alouatta* makes more noise for its size than any other animal on our planet. Its popular name, not without reason, is the howler monkey.

I first became intimately acquainted with howlers in the 1950s, when the State Department chose to ignore my patient studies of the Russian language and assigned me as cultural attaché to the United States Embassy in Guatemala, Central America. Not long after my arrival, just as the country began to recover from one of its periodic revolutions, there came to the embassy a Yale University graduate and career foreign service officer with the mellisonant name of Wymberly De Renne Coerr. Wymberly, as I always respectfully addressed him, was to be our new deputy chief of mission and held the rank of Counselor of Embassy. Although I was some years his junior and many grades below him, he very soon singled me out as his traveling companion for what he called outings in the Guatemalan countryside. I usually felt pleased and not a little flattered when this happened, but I realize now that his invitations were more the result of his being unable to find anyone else in the embassy community willing to accompany him. This was because his outings were often long and frequently arduous trips to remote or difficult places.

I was not altogether surprised, then, when Wymberly proposed we paddle down the Polochic River in the tropical rain forest of the remote Alta Verapaz province in eastern

Guatemala. The Polochic, he explained, would take us to Guatemala's large inland sea, known as Lake Izabal. Once there we would have to paddle across Izabal's 25-mile length to the narrow and canyonlike Rio Dulce, which would eventually bring us out to the small port of Livingston on the Caribbean Sea. By his rough estimate, it was a trip of slightly more than a hundred miles.

At first I demurred, not only because of the trip's length but also because I had not yet fully recovered from climbing Guatemala's 12,300-foot Agua volcano, one of Wymberly's "outings," which in my view proved to be something closer to a major mountaineering expedition. When I told Wymberly my knee was still sore from a fall I had taken during our midnight ascent—he had insisted that we reach Agua's summit by dawn for maximum visibility—he politely reminded me that hiking would be no part of our jungle outing. We would be sitting in his kayak all the while, and, what was more, he would bear the brunt of any portages or heavy lifting that might be required. It was as simple as that.

Central to Wymberly's proposal were Chris Hempstead, an expatriate friend of mine who piloted a Piper Cub, and Wymberly's Klepper Folbot, a collapsible two-seater kayak introduced to the United States shortly after World War II and now recognized as the progenitor of many river-running models by today's legions of kayakers. The Piper Cub could take us reasonably near to the Rio Polochic, and the Folbot, we sincerely hoped, down the long and various waterways to the sea. Moreover, what was equally important, Chris Hempstead knew the way to the Alta Verapaz, which was then a largely trackless and thinly populated expanse of tropical rain forest. His Hempstead family forebears, he told us, had been among the first to settle the region as coffee planters and had in fact cleared a small aircraft landing strip not too far from the Polochic. Accordingly, on a fine morning of the chosen day at the start of the dry season, we set off in the Piper from the Guatemala City airport. The little plane took off rather sluggishly, I thought, probably because every cubic inch of the cabin interior and the luggage compartment in the tail section was crammed with the Folbot parts, jungle hammocks, and other camping gear, not to mention all our food and drink supplies.

What I remember most from the first leg of our journey was the realization that the Guatemalan dry season meant *relatively* dry, or in some parts of the country, not dry at all. Very soon, as we flew through a mountain pass in the Sierra de las Minas range northeast of Guatemala City, Chris began to twist and turn the Piper between huge columns of cumulus clouds that were now rising from the mountains below. As we did so I spotted another small plane below us, traveling in the opposite direction. The sight of this plane, so tiny and insignificant against the backdrop of the rising cloud masses, was both impressive and sobering. Most of the clouds were blindingly white, but some were already steel-wool gray in their lower parts, casting down dark curtains of rain. Any one of them, we knew, might soon be forming thunderheads which would hold in their cores enough violent drafts to wreck small aircraft. We wagged our wings at the other plane, which returned the gesture. Thus reassured, we flew on.

We soon cleared the mountain pass and came into calm air and blue skies. Below us was a dense canopy of green broken only by the silvery reflection of mountain streams tumbling their way down to the Rio Polochic. It was my first aerial view of a tropical rain forest and it seemed to me the green carpet of its canopy was endless, extending as far as the eye could see in every direction. Not long thereafter, however, Chris announced that we were reaching the Hempstead family *finca*.

Below us was a sizable plantation home surrounded by a grove of coffee bushes and their ubiquitous shade trees. Within this grove clustered around the *casa grande* were various outbuildings, a native village, and a neatly painted schoolhouse. About a half-mile away from this complex was a grass landing strip hacked out of the forest. Here Chris landed with a deft touch, meaning with hardly a noticeable bounce. Almost immediately the Piper was surrounded by friendly *peones* who hailed "Don Cris" and offered to take our luggage to the big house, where some refreshments awaited us. But Wymberly, who I have always thought had a clock in his head, politely declined the invitation saying there were only six hours of daylight left and that we had to get well down the river if we wanted to reach Lake Izabal the next day.

Approximately two hours later we managed to squeeze ourselves into the Folbot seats and launch ourselves on the Polochic. No time had been wasted in rest or idle gazing by the riverside, much as we might have wanted to do so. As any reader who has owned a Folbot will understand, it had taken us more than an hour to assemble and fine-tune the kayak under a broiling sun.

This done, we had found to our dismay that less than half of our gear and supplies would fit under the forward and aft canvas decking of the Folbot. Wymberly therefore laid out everything we had brought on the riverbank and began what he called an equipment triage. Everything he deemed absolutely essential went into one pile. Everything he thought was not, into another, which soon grew larger. Among the latter were three large jugs of spring water and two cases of bottled drinks which Wymberly said were too heavy and took up too much space. We would simply have to fill our canteens with river water, add halazone pills, and shake vigorously. Thus treated, the Polochic water would be quite safe, Wymberly insisted. The embassy doctor had told him so, in fact. Among the essentials were foodstuffs, first-aid kits, a change of clothes, and jungle hammocks, the latter being included only after much debate. As events would prove, this was the wisest decision of our trip.

Now at last we were off. The Folbot surged easily ahead with each of Wymberly's powerful strokes. Helping us along was the Polochic's swift current which swirled around the Folbot, making little whorls in the clear tea-colored water. By Wymberly's leave I sat relaxed in the bow—we would change places later—eating a sandwich my wife had made early that morning and drinking the only bottle of cold soda I had filched from the triage.

Our downstream paddle was at first pure bliss. We moved swiftly between the walls of the Polochic's gallery forest, with dense green masses of vegetation rising on each side of us from water's edge to heights of 200 feet. As a result Wymberly for once seemed to have forgotten the clock in his head. He had stopped paddling and sat idly gazing at the green walls in an attitude that was almost reverential. In this manner we drifted happily downriver, almost effortlessly and silently. The only sounds were occasional bird cries and drops of water falling from our resting paddles.

First impressions of a tropical rain forest are almost as varied as those who experience them. One that stands out in my mind, especially in relation to our trip on the Polochic, comes from the writer Diane Ackerman. "No emptiness goes unfilled," she has observed. "No gap of sunlight goes untrapped."

Surprises came with almost every bend in the river. But true to Ms. Ackerman's description, it required close attention and a sharp eye to find them. You might catch a little beam of trapped sunlight behind the gallery's facade and find it occupied by a dainty white egret picking its way between a tangle of roots and vines. Above it, quietly occupying a branch that barely protrudes beyond the green wall, there sits a small kingfisher recognizable only by its silhouette, not by its diminutive size or its bold tropical colors. Beneath the kingfisher an alligator lies motionless in the dark water. Typically only his eyes and nostrils show above the surface. Just above it on a bare branch is a basilisk lizard, as immobile as a statue. Sensing our approach the lizard darts out onto the water and runs pitter-patter on its surface, legs flailing wildly until it submerges at a safe distance away. Not without reason the basilisk is known in Spanish as the *Jesu Cristo lagarto,* or "Jesus lizard."

Far too soon our idyllic float came to an abrupt halt. The river course grew wide, with a corresponding loss of current, and a strong head wind buffeted the Folbot. As a result we were no longer able to drift or even glide with easy paddle strokes. More than that, if we stopped paddling, we lost ground. With Wymberly urging me on like a coxswain on a varsity crew, we put all our strength in each stroke. Gone were any more opportunities to view the forest wildlife, except for a noisy flight of small green parrots. Almost as if to taunt us, they flew right over our heads and straight downstream at a speed we could only watch and envy.

Happily some ugly-looking storm clouds soon faded away to the east and the gallery forest closed in to give us more shelter. Now we could drift again. I pulled out my canteen, filled it with river water, and shook vigorously. The first taste was a shock, but I soon found myself drinking heavily, so great was my thirst. Wymberly, I noticed, soon did the same.

Just as we sat discussing the respective strength of our halazone cocktails, we heard a strange roaring noise. It seemed to come from a great distance.

"What in the world was that?" I asked, not really expecting a definitive answer.

"Probably howler monkeys," Wymberly answered matter-of-factly. He thought he remembered hearing them in Honduras, where he was first posted as a career foreign service officer. "They say you can hear them a mile away."

Monkeys, I thought to myself, could not possibly make such a noise. The distant roars sounded more like a pack of lions, a pack of lions with indigestion, that is. At the very least the roaring had to come from a large mammal. Jaguars were known to inhabit the forests of Alta Verapaz and the neighboring province of El Petén. But jaguars and other of the tropical forest cats are solitary in habit and never given to hunting or traveling in packs. That much I knew.

Not long after the strange roars we heard an airplane engine in the distance. Moments later Chris Hempstead flew over us in the Piper. He then turned around and buzzed us very low on a second pass. By prearrangement, we made hand signals to indicate all was well with us. Chris wagged his wings in recognition, turned sharply to the south, and headed homeward.

Chris's buzz and the helpful river current buoyed our spirits. Darkness soon came, a full moon slowly climbed up from the horizon, and the cool of the evening came on as a blessed relief from the damp heat of the day. We passed one or two clearings in the gallery forest where we might have stopped for the night, but Wymberly said we were making such good time that it seemed a shame to stop. Exhilarated, I agreed.

However, after an hour of swift progress, we became quite concerned. We had not seen one clearing, not one landing place all the while. At one point we passed a midstream gravel bar, which I thought looked promising. But there were crocodiles and alligators to think about and no trees for hanging our hammocks. Besides, as Wymberly was quick to point out, heavy rains upstream could crest during the night and sweep us away.

Finally, around what I think was eleven o'clock that night, we found a gap in one of the river's green walls. We immediately landed and were cheered to find a small clearing with firm ground. There then followed one of the worst moments of the trip.

Within seconds of landing, even as we were dragging the Folbot up the riverbank, a dense cloud of mosquitoes attacked us. We did not even have the satisfaction of swatting at them since our hands were almost continuously occupied with unpacking our gear and the difficult task of rigging our jungle hammocks. The mosquitoes bit us again and again, relentlessly. Insect repellent was of no use, nor did our clothing provide much protection. The mosquitoes bit through our sweat-soaked shirts and even on occasion our damp trousers.

For obvious reasons we skipped the solace of a proper supper. I opened a can of beef ravioli, stuffed some crackers in my pocket, and carefully placed my canteen, the canned ravioli, a dry shirt, and our one bottle of Scotch whisky (after offering Wymberly a swig) inside my hammock. Then, when all seemed ready, I unzipped one of the hammock's side panels for most of its length, stripped off my wet shirt, and climbed in as cautiously as possible. (As those familiar with jungle hammocks will know, a rash entry can easily upset the hammock, with the result that the occupant is then trapped like a fish in a net and may even require help to get out.) I got in successfully, in short, but so did too many mosquitoes. From what I remember, I next spent a long time alternately munching crackers, gulping ravioli, swigging halazone water, and taking Scotch whisky inside and out, meaning both swallowing it and rubbing small amounts on my lacerated body. Occasionally, I think, there were also some brief moments of sleep.

After one such moment, perhaps four or five hours later,

I opened a bleary eye to a gray dawn. Almost at the same time I was roused from my comatose state by an utterly strange and fearful noise. It began as a series of rhythmic hoots and grunts, then culminated in loud and deep-throated roars. After one such sequence it came to me that the roars had to come from the celebrated howlers Wymberly had mentioned. Without moving from my hammock, I guessed that they were very close at hand. In fact I could hear the howlers, if that was indeed what they were, sucking in air with each hoot, much like singers storing up breath for a long solo passage. Then came the hoots and roars, often in a deafening chorus.

"Are you awake?" Wymberly now asked me.

"Are you out of your head, Wym," I answered, for once forgetting the deferential manner in which I normally addressed him. "Of course I'm awake!"

"I think they're throwing things at me," Wymberly added.

I told Wymberly to try to get more sleep; meanwhile I would get up and investigate. Immediately upon extricating myself from my hammock, I looked up at the treetops that bordered our tiny clearing.

There they were, about 12 or more large black monkeys, obviously excited by our presence. Those nearest to me were the largest and the most agitated, running back and forth on the stoutest branches. They either bared their teeth at me or pouted their lips in perfectly rounded circles as they began their hoots and grunts. Then came the great roaring, with a number of the monkeys sounding off in unison. As I prepared to retreat, I saw one monkey vigorously shaking a branch. Another nearby snapped off some branches and let them drop near Wymberly's hammock, which was deeper in under the trees than mine. The twigs fell short, but I could see that some were right on the mark, on top of the hammock rain fly. Thus Wymberly's concern about "throwing things at me."

I reported to Wymberly that our neighbors were howlers all right, no doubt about it, and then carefully reentered my hammock. Perhaps the howling would stop if we were both very quiet, I thought to myself.

Unfortunately, it did not. If anything, the howling grew louder, with what seemed like more voices joining the chorus.

"I can't stand this anymore," Wymberly now said. "Let's break camp."

"For God's sake, let's get a little more rest," I insisted. "They can't keep this up very much longer."

I could not have been more mistaken. On and on came the howls, booming out over the forest. First, the now familiar hoots and grunts, then the loud roars. I cannot say how long this episode lasted. Perhaps it was no more than 10 or 15 minutes. But under the circumstances it seemed an eternity.

There are many occasions when howler monkeys howl, but

none is more sure to occur than at dawn, at which time the howling may indeed be prolonged and loud. It has nothing to do with a good-morning greeting, however, or any other manifestation of cordiality. Rather, what is happening is that the howlers feel impelled to start the day by announcing their whereabouts, by saying in effect "we are here, we are here" to their neighbors.

Howler monkeys normally move about in troops of approximately 15 to 20 individuals through what are small areas in the upper stories of the forests. These ranges, as they are more properly called, frequently overlap. If indeed two troops are in an overlap area or anywhere near each other, they will exchange howls for as long as one or the other believes necessary to avoid conflict. A space defense mechanism is what some scientists prefer to call this early morning ritual, as well as certain other regular howling occasions. They serve the useful purpose of preventing close troop encounters, which nearly always result in face-offs—ferocious howling matches, that is to say—and may last for hours, time much better spent in feeding and rest.

When at last the howling stopped, Wymberly gave me no argument about the need to pause and prepare a substantial breakfast. Happily the hordes of mosquitoes of the night before were not yet to be seen or felt. We therefore took the trouble to break out our little Sterno stove and warm up a can of corned beef hash, some tortillas, and a cup or two of instant coffee. Meanwhile our friends high up in the cecropia trees gradually calmed down and watched us in silence.

Howler troops are quick to recognize field scientists and other observers who visit their home ranges with some frequency. The monkeys therefore do not howl or show other signs of excitation at the sight of such familiar visitors. I can only suppose that the same holds true for strangers who settle down quietly to their own business and pay the monkeys no heed. This, at least, is the only way I can explain our peaceful breakfast hour and the howlers' silent departure.

The odd-sounding grunts we heard just before the troop left, I have since learned, were in fact a distinctive signal in the howlers' ample repertoire of vocalizations. It usually occurs when the troop's leading male decides it is time to move to more tempting fruits and other treetop delights. After he voices his intention with the low grunts, the troop will dutifully follow him, single file, over the stoutest branches. They move slowly and with caution, as befits *Alouatta pigra*, or the black howler of Central America, which is the largest and heaviest of New World primates. (Adult males weigh 16 to 20 pounds; females, 13 to 15.) As they do so, one or two in the troop, usually males, will begin howling. Again they are exercising space defense. Now they are saying, "we are moving, we are moving."

Another occasion when howler monkeys nearly always howl is the sudden arrival of rain, either as a tropical cloudburst or a steady downpour. Since the annual rainfall in most of the tropical regions inhabited by howlers runs from 200 to 300 inches a year, such a reaction seems a paradox, or at the very least, curious. Those who have frequently observed it believe it is more a complaint at the noise—of a thunderclap, say, or heavy rain splattering on large leaves—than at the discomfort of getting a little wet. Buttressing this view is the fact that in the days not long ago when aircraft were smaller and flew at lower altitudes, howlers were often seen roaring defiance at the first sounds of engine noise.

As might be expected, there have been many attempts to describe the full-bodied roar of *Alouatta*. I like best that of the late Frank Chapman, an ornithologist of a previous generation whose broad interests extended to all that surrounded him in the natural world. Chapman, a staff scientist at the American Museum of Natural History, once lived for an extended period in what he liked to call his "tropical air castle," or a secluded cabin almost underneath a resident troop of howlers on the Smithsonian Institution's Barro Colorado Island in the Panama Canal Zone. "Beginning as a slow grunt, it grows louder, more rapid, more incisive, and quickly rises to an overpowering ferocious-sounding roar," Dr. Chapman has written. "A single Howler might challenge a Lion to a vocal duel with every hope of victory; when a band of Howlers join forces the Lion may well retire from the field. . . . A Howler chorus is one of the most impressive sounds in the animal world."

Earlier attempts to describe the howlers' roars, we may note in passing, have used emotive terms as "harrowing" and "frightful." Others have given up and simply called them "insufferable and indescribable."

The organ that provides the howlers with their vocal prowess has been described as "an enormous distension of the body of the hyoid bone into a large, deep bony cup, sheltered between the two jaws which are especially deep for that purpose." Indeed, the sounding chamber which this bony cup provides barely fits between the monkey's jaws and extends below them. The size of a large plum, it helps to give the howlers their characteristic jowly appearance. By contrast the human hyoid bone is thin, delicate, and quite small. It does not function as a resonator.

Given such equipment it is no wonder that some scientists have flatly declared that *Alouatta*'s howls "are considered to be the loudest sound animals are capable of producing." Supporting this claim is the fact that under favorable conditions howler choruses have been heard in tests at a distance of two miles or more.

Its remarkable vocalizations aside, *Alouatta pigra* has not fared well at the hands of early voyagers and natural philosophers. Capt. William Dampier, the literate 17th-century buccaneer who once held a commission from the British Admiralty, has left us with a vivid and in many ways remarkably accurate description of his first encounter with howler troops in Central America:

The Monkies that are in these Parts are the ugliest I ever saw. . . . They were a large Company dancing from Tree to Tree, over my Head; chattering and making a terrible Noise; and a great many grim Faces, and shewing antick Gestures. Some broke down dry Sticks and threw at me; others scattered their Urine and Dung about my Ears; at last one bigger than the rest, came to a small Limb just over my Head; and leaping directly at me, made me start back; but the Monkie caught hold of the Bough with the tip of his Tail; and there continued swinging to and fro, and making Mouths at me. . . . These Monkies are the most sullen I ever met with; for all the Art we could use would never tame them. . . . [They] are very rarely, or (as some say) never on the Ground.

To which we may add the more recent observations of Frank Chapman, who had this to say about the oldest male in the troop that lived almost directly above his cabin on Barro Colorado Island:

I have seen him roar and I have seen him yawn, I have seen him awake and also asleep, and the sum total of my impression is that his face is the incarnation of every evil thought that has ever passed through the mind of man. Large, round, sooty black eyes, deep-set, far apart, and overhung by a low forehead, nose so flat that it is little more than a site for the nostrils, mouth so enormous that when widely opened the head disappears behind gaping rows of teeth, a scraggly beard, the whole expression an inconceivable exaggeration of gloomy, bestial brutality.

The troop that William Dampier met with exhibited the typical "rage" and "fright" behavior that occurs upon meeting humans, other threatening animals, or another troop. The running to and fro on tree branches, the grim faces of the largest males as they bare their teeth or pout their lips, the cacophony of their grunts and roars, and the defecation and urination upon intruders have all been frequently witnessed by present-day scientists. In the latter case C. R. Carpenter, a Yale University professor of psychology, who like Chapman studied howlers on Barro Colorado in the 1930s, has provided the most interesting examples. "I would usually be sitting quietly observing the animals as they were in the trees above me," Carpenter has written. "Either seen or unseen, an individual would slowly approach to a place directly above me, or as near as possible, and then would release excrement, either urine or fecal matter or both. When the act was completed, the individual would usually quickly withdraw." Not content with such examples of individual behavior, Dr. Carpenter then constructed a blind under a troop's line of march. The result was much the same. "I have seen as many as half of the animals release fecal matter on the blind as they crossed over," Carpenter writes. "The animals would stop, complete the act, and then hurriedly continue." From all such experiences he cautiously concluded that there was "a certain directedness about this behavior." Readers, I am sure, will agree.

But spectacular as the howling and confrontational displays of a troop may be, the more admirable characteristics of troop behavior are just as interesting and in some cases unique. Dampier, for example, was quick to note that mothers typically carried their young on their backs whenever necessary, especially when "the Females with their young are much troubled to leap after the Males." Although mothers among many other primate species will help juveniles cross gaps between branches, it is probably more difficult for the heavy-bodied howlers, who do not like to jump. Many, therefore, are the contemporary field observations of mothers making living bridges across spaces that their young could not manage by themselves. In some cases mothers will indeed jump, holding the terminal twigs of one branch by their tails and leaping as much as four feet to grasp another. They will then hold the bridge they have thus made with their bodies and tails for as long as a minute or more, until the juvenile or infant is encouraged to cross on it. This done, mother and child will continue on their own.

By the same token when infants or crippled adults lag behind in the course of travel, one or another of the leading males will make a distinctive distress vocalization. This will be clearly understood by the other troop members, who will then dutifully stop and wait for the disadvantaged to catch up.

Frank Chapman tells of how he once heard males roaring and females emitting strange noises he had never heard before, all for no reason that he could determine. Presently, however, he discovered a howler infant, perhaps no more than a week or two old, that had fallen to the ground. The baby was obviously sick, with most of its body covered with botfly larvae and other sores.

As it cried, the troop sat overhead while the mother several times descended close to the ground. But in each instance her nerve failed her and she climbed back up to rejoin her troop. For six hours the mother and a male, probably the baby's father, kept up their vigil, the baby crying and the mother answering with a curious moaning sound. "The baby was [by] now in a dying condition," Chapman concluded. "Its life ended painlessly and the clan disappeared in the forest to the west."

Similarly, Professor Carpenter once heard an object fall to the ground, followed almost instantly by roaring and eerie wailing sounds. He soon found a baby howler lying on the forest floor, stunned and bleeding from the nose. As he approached it, the troop as a whole climbed down closer to the ground, while the mother descended to within 25 feet of her child and started pulling on vines that hung nearest to it. By this time the child, somewhat recovered, was making attempts to reach these vines. But Dr. Carpenter evidently could not resist the opportunity for close observation of an animal so difficult to capture and keep. "I prevented the infant from climbing back into the tree, although it was constantly striving to climb upwards," he has written. "Never did the males cease roaring. After half an hour I took the infant and carried it away while the

mother followed me for several hundred yards, wailing piti-
fully in response to the distress cries of the infant."

Apart from parental concern, these two and many other
accounts demonstrate what every student of *Alouatta* soon
understands; namely, that howler monkeys are among the
most arboreal of all primates, so much so that they rarely if
ever descend to the ground. They are born, they live, and
they die high up in the towering ficus and cecropia trees
that provide their choicest fare. Helping them in their treetop existence—indeed, essential to it—is the howler's tail.
Measuring three and a half to four feet, it is as long as the
howler's body and head combined and has at the underside
of its tip four to five inches of hairless and extremely sensi-
tive skin. Often called a fifth limb or more commonly a
third hand, the tail and its prehensile tip can give the
howlers a great advantage in foraging. As often as not, they
may be seen hanging by their tails while both their hands
seek out the fruits and leaves of the season. Equally important, a howler monkey will never sleep or rest without first
firmly anchoring its tail around a supporting tree limb. So
firm is the tail's grasp that hunters sometimes cannot
recover howlers they have killed, as both Dampier and
Chapman have recorded, since they hang "tied to branches
beyond reach by the convulsive grip of a circle of bone,
muscle, and sinew that relaxes only in decay."

Thus equipped, it is small wonder that howlers have no
use for terra firma and its many predators. The one

exception—better said, the only circumstance—that forces them to do otherwise is the partial or total destruction of their arboreal habitat. Faced with consequent hunger, howler troops will gingerly descend to the ground and set off in a clumsy quadrupedal gait in search of greener treetop mansions.

Wymberly and I had no opportunity to see this or any other howler monkey phenomena, much as we might have wished to. It was necessary to push on, to use Wymberly's most constant reminder, if ever we were to reach the Caribbean.

My memory of the rest of the trip is at best hazy. At the mouth of the Rio Polochic where it meets Lake Izabal, we chose the wrong arm of the river's marshy delta and had to backtrack, often against current and wind, to find our way out. Wymberly, who was powerfully built in his upper torso, paddled vigorously and without complaint. By contrast I felt weary, dehydrated, and feeble. A night of negligible sleep and the now hot sun were taking their toll.

What stands out, however, is one brief and very exciting moment. When at last we saw the great expanse of Lake Izabal not far ahead, I noticed that Wymberly's spirits were brightening, and I seized the opportunity to ask him if we might not pause in the lee of the last stand of tall marsh grass and try a little fishing. (I had saved my small spinning rod from the equipment triage, claiming it might be needed as a source of emergency food supply.) Wymberly agreed and on my third cast a very large *robalo*—well known as snook to Florida sportfishermen—hit my plug in a shimmering jump. It was in truth a big robalo weighing at least ten pounds by conservative estimate, the like of which I have not since seen or caught. True to form, it fought hard, jumping repeatedly, until it soon tired. But as I drew the robalo closer to the kayak, I saw that its size presented a problem. Wymberly, who was in the rear seat, said he refused to have a big fish thrashing around his bare legs and splattering blood all over his prized Folbot. For my part, I could not very well squeeze the fish in under the forward canvas decking, which was entirely occupied by camping gear and our spare clothes, not to mention my legs.

"Besides, how could we ever cook it on the little Sterno?" Wymberly now asked. "We have to push on," he added once again.

I carefully unhooked my beautiful fish. It was gratifying, after all, to see it swim away unharmed and in good condition.

But another very exciting moment—exciting to me, at least—soon followed. We had not paddled for more than a mile, battling head winds that were already dusting up small whitecaps, when I became obsessed with the thought that we could not possibly traverse the 25-mile length of the big lake without one or possibly two more nights in the bush. As far as we could see, there was not a sign of human habitation anywhere along the vastness of Lake Izabal's green shores, although we were told that small villages of the secretive Kekchi Indians were in some places hidden in the forest behind the shoreline. But even as I mulled over these dismal prospects, civilization appeared in the form of a small speck on the horizon. As the speck grew larger we saw it was a 40-foot motor launch with a sturdy shade roof, a small pilot house, and room enough for about a dozen passengers and assorted freight. The launch immediately changed course to intercept us, and its captain hailed us in a friendly tone as soon as his voice could carry over the wind. He invited us to come aboard, Folbot and all.

"*Gracias, muchísimas gracias,*" I immediately shouted back, before Wymberly had any chance to refuse.

Once aboard, the captain told us that Don Chris Hempstead had told him to look out for two gringos in a strange-looking little boat. The launch made biweekly trips from Panzós, a small town far up the Polochic River, all the way down to Livingston on the Caribbean, stopping wherever there might be any passengers or small freight. We were welcome to stay aboard as long as we wanted. Don Chris was *muy caballero,* the captain added, a real gentleman whom he was always pleased to serve.

We stopped at the ruins of the Castillo de San Felipe at the eastern end of Lake Izabal, about 18 miles from where we had been picked up. Here we put up in a hostelry with a single malodorous bathroom. I am told that I slumped over the dinner table and fell into what seemed either deep sleep or a fainting spell. Only the next morning did I learn that Wymberly had dispatched the genial launch captain, who was by then well on his way to Livingston.

In retrospect I am glad that Wymberly did this. In time, or after further tribulations and much hard paddling, we came to the narrows of the Rio Dulce, which is in effect a continuation of the Polochic, picking up as it does at the other end of Lake Izabal. But perhaps it is well that the Rio Dulce—the River Sweet—has an identity all its own, for along its lower course lies one of the great scenic wonders of Central America. In 1841 John Lloyd Stephens, the New York lawyer-turned-explorer, described the Dulce narrows in his *Incidents of Travel in Central America, Chiapas, and Yucatan,* as "a fairy scene of Titan land, combining exquisite beauty with colossal grandeur. . . . On each side, rising perpendicularly from three hundred to four hundred feet was a wall of living green. Trees grew from the water's edge, with dense, unbroken foliage, to the top. . . ."

Indeed, the canyonlike gorge of the Dulce was every bit as grand and as awe inspiring as Stephens had described it, except for one important detail. The walls that rose perpendicularly for 300 or 400 feet were bare stone, light gray in color and free of any dense vegetation, much less trees growing from the water's edge. The effect if anything was more impressive. It was as though we had entered the nave of a huge gray-stone cathedral, with only a narrow band of blue sky for its roof. The silence that enveloped us was almost palpable. We stopped paddling and said not a word.

The Dulce meandered thus for three or four miles within the great walls. We saw not another boat until about halfway through, where we found two Kekchi Indians fishing from a sturdy dugout canoe. Coming closer, we were amazed to see a large dead bull shark* occupying most of the dugout's interior. It was at least nine feet in length, or so long that the better part of its tail drooped over the edge of the nearly swamped dugout. Here a little remora swam back and forth, never more than inches from the shark's tail, with the sucking disk on the top of its head plainly exposed. The remora was puzzled, I imagined, wondering why its host was not moving through the water and providing the usual fish scraps from its prey.

Not long thereafter I tried a few more casts with my spinning rod. On the third or fourth cast a huge silvery tarpon hit my lure in an astonishing leap. It sailed high up into the air—gills flaring, its head shaking fiercely—so high and so close to the boat, in fact, that Wymberly and I both ducked for fear it might land on us. The tarpon obliged, however, by hitting the water, not us, with a resounding splash that sent wavelets racing across the Dulce. My line went limp, as I fully expected. Moments later I got the feeling I had done something wrong. It was not right to disturb the peace in

---

* *Carcharhinus leucas* is a large and dangerous shark that favors coastal embayments and estuaries. It tolerates both fresh and salt water and can also be found in greater numbers in Lake Nicaragua, along with the sawfish.

this way, I began to think, to violate as it were the sanctum of our private cathedral. I put the rod away.

The Rio Dulce returned to its glassy calm. Once again the silence was overwhelming, broken only by our paddle strokes and the cries of distant birds. We traveled easily and swiftly for what I hoped were miles on end. Moments later Wymberly confirmed my most optimistic estimate of our progress. After studying his map, he boldly announced that we were not far from Livingston and the Caribbean Sea. True, his map was small in scale, embracing nearly all of Guatemala, but good enough to gauge relative distances, Wymberly thought.

As we were congratulating ourselves on this encouraging estimate, we heard a sound that seemed to come from far, far away. Now we both smiled. It sounded for all the world like the distant roaring of a pack of lions. But this time we knew. It was our good friends, the howlers. That, indeed, is how we now liked to think of them. Even from our brief introductory meeting back on the Polochic, we both sensed that all the "rage" manifestations we had witnessed—the running to and fro, the throwing of branches, the pouting of lips, and the full chorus of the roars—had nothing to do with any particular animus toward us. Rather, all these actions were but a show designed mainly to make us keep our distance. And as Wymberly now pointed out, when we went quietly about our business, so too did the howlers. In fact you could almost think of them as peaceable animals, he added.

Just how peaceable, if that is the right word, is a matter of debate among field scientists who know howlers best. Early studies, notably those of the Yale psychologist C. R. Carpenter in the 1930s, characterized the howlers' behavior within their troops as "generally peaceful and cooperative." In fact Carpenter claimed never to have seen howlers, even the largest males, fight over or attempt to steal food, granted their food supply is usually plentiful. Moreover, Carpenter believed that the absence of pugnacious behavior, which he found rarely if ever occurred within the troop, was essential to the howlers' high degree of group cohesion. "The characteristic relations among males and the lack of a sharp gradient of dominance and submission," he concluded, "are necessary to the type of communal grouping found."

Similarly Frank Chapman, the same Frank Chapman who once described the old male of the troop that lived above his cabin on Barro Colorado as the incarnation "of gloomy, bestial brutality," eventually came around to describing troop behavior in the most Elysian terms. "Life within the clan appears to be wholly peaceful," he has written. "Neither by word nor deed have I observed any evidence of anger or selfishness."

More recently Katherine Milton of the University of California, who has studied howlers on Barro Colorado Island since 1974, has discovered that each troop does indeed have a dominant male and a male hierarchy based mainly on age. But this hierarchy is never as forcefully expressed as, for example, that of Old World baboons. In fact it is usually confined to the privilege of associating with females and infants, associations that are denied the younger males. What is more, Dr. Milton has witnessed fights when the latter seek to improve their status by moving in on their elders. These fights can turn vicious, causing serious wounds or even death in the event one or the other contestant falls to the ground.

Still and all, there is agreement among nearly all observers, Dr. Milton included, that howler monkeys live generally peaceful lives. For all their ferocious appearance, males routinely allow infants to sit on their heads or explore their facial features, all without a word or sign of reproach. And it is also true that males cooperate, as for example in exploring new routes for safe travel along the tree limbs of their aerial habitat. Then, too, the howlers' roars—the very act of roaring so essential to spatial defense—may be counted as a form of cooperation or at least unity of purpose. Preliminary grunts aside, the rhythmic roaring that can carry two miles is always started on cue, with all the males joining in to make a synchronous, full-bodied chorus.

There is yet another feature of howler behavior that seems to provide the perfect image of peaceful existence, although some may prefer to call it indolence. In an exhaustive study of the howlers' daily rounds, Dr. Milton found that the Barro Colorado howlers spent almost two-thirds of the day—65.5 percent of the daylight hours, to be exact—at rest. They are able to do so because their food supply, if not always their favorite fruits, is relatively plentiful and usually not far away. Thus they can meet their nutritional requirements after only three or four hours of foraging every day.

So it is that you will often find a howler troop lazing away most of the day in a favored tree. Predictably, it will be one that provides wild fig or other choice delicacies and a leafy canopy that offers some shelter from torrential rains. All the troop members will be there. Mothers will settle into the fork of a limb and tend to their infants. Males will find a broad tree crotch and claim it for most of the rest period. Juveniles swing by their tails and play-fight. It is indeed a peaceful, homelike scene, one that with care you may observe without disturbance. But as Wymberly correctly inferred, you must go quietly about your own business. Make one threatening gesture or step one pace in the wrong direction and you may be forced to flee. Your ears will be assaulted by the sound that even scientists have pronounced "insufferable." Your head will ache should you choose to hold your ground, for the howlers will easily outlast you in patience, continuing their chorus for hours on end.

Heard from a distance the howlers' great roars are not unpleasant. We should think of them as part of the tropical rain forest's diurnal symphony of sounds. To hear their roars is cause to rejoice, in fact, for they are a sign that all is well for the moment in the world's richest and most significant biome.

For the moment. How much longer this will hold true is a difficult question. It is now 45 years since Wymberly and I successfully completed our Guatemalan outing and I have not had many subsequent opportunities to hear the howlers' calls, much less meet them at such close quarters as at our campsite on the Polochic River—nor has Wymberly, it grieves me to say, who has only recently passed on to his ultimate and richly deserved rewards.

I would especially like to see *Alouatta* again by retracing our route down the Polochic, across Izabal, and through the Dulce narrows. But I cannot find it in my heart to revisit the region. A recent English-language guidebook to Central America describes the tourist hub of El Relleno, also known as Rio Dulce, as being in the center of "a spectacularly beautiful [area] . . . currently undergoing steady development" and recommends several "upmarket hotels offering luxurious accommodations." The same guide speaks of the area around the Castillo de San Felipe and the eastern end of Lake Izabal as "a favorite playground for wealthy Guatemalans, with boats and hotels that would put parts of California to shame." Cruise ships working the Caribbean and Central America have recently begun to include Livingston and the Rio Dulce in their itineraries.

Resort development is but one small factor of a complex

global problem. The problem, as readers surely know, is loss of habitat. It is especially acute in the tropical rain forests so essential to the survival of the howlers and a multitude of other plant and animal species. These forests alone—the tropical rain forests of the Western Hemisphere, that is— are being cut down or burned up at the alarming rate of over 100,000 acres a day. Roads crisscross even the most remote strands, opening them up to timber cruising, mining, and, worst of all, the ruinous and self-defeating practice of slash-and-burn agriculture. Even as these lines are written, forests are aflame in the greater part of Mexico and Central America, sending a pall of smoke over Texas and parts of the Midwest. And the evening news announces that in Mexico some of the forests have been set ablaze by drug suppliers and runners anxious to erase their tracks. The official explanation is an extraordinary dry season, brought on by the vagaries of El Niño, as were the floods of the winter wet season, of course.

Thus if you would be sure to see howlers today, you are best advised to head for nature reserves or other protected areas such as Barra Honda National Park and the Cabo Blanco Biological Reserve in Costa Rica or the Baboon Community Sanctuary in Belize. There are also well maintained private reserves at resorts specializing in ecotourism, such as Lapa Rios in Costa Rica or Chan Chich in interior Belize. Or should you have the necessary scientific credentials, there is always Barro Colorado, the Smithsonian's venerable tropical research center in the Panama Canal Zone. Now as before it remains an excellent study area for the howler monkey, not to mention such other primates as the spider and night monkeys or larger mammals such as the tapir and both the white-lipped and white-collared peccaries.

I have a vision—a haunting vision I find hard to dismiss—that stems from one of Frank Chapman's most memorable experiences during his residences at Barro Colorado. It happened that Chapman was put in charge of a two-month-old female howler, another victim of a tree fall, at the island's research station. Very quickly he developed a strong affection for the young howler, whom he named Claudia, describing her as having "large, luminous, intelligent, in fact, human black eyes . . . [with which] she regarded you with a spirit of calm, discriminating independence." After a somewhat difficult trial period Chapman achieved what William Dampier, native Americans, and many field scientists have long failed to do—namely, to establish a degree of trust and friendship with a howler monkey. Chapman's friendship in fact developed to such a point that Claudia would jump to greet him every time he entered her spacious cage, leaving even her food to do so. But as Chapman made clear, Claudia might be counted a friend but never a pet. Moreover, even though their friendship developed rapidly, it was strictly "on Claudia's lines; and Claudia's lines were play, more play, and harder play."

Under these terms the friendship grew, the more so when Chapman wore a heavy wool sock for Claudia to chew, draped over one hand, leaving his other hand free for the rough and tumble play she so enjoyed. But there was one dark cloud—better said, a barrier—that their friendship never overcame. Chapman's diary tells us:

> This afternoon Claudia howled continually for at least half an hour. Evidently she was startled by hearing some of her kind, but they were so far away that one had to listen intently to hear them. She jumped from limb to limb of her tree angrily shaking its branches with her hands and even biting them.
>
> Claudia is wild and restless. She calls constantly and rushes about her cage floor, always on the forest side, as though looking for a way out. . . . She was not still for thirty consecutive seconds during the day.
>
> As before this activity was caused by hearing howlers call. Then would follow a period when there were no other howlers in our vicinity and Claudia seemed wholly reconciled to cage-life. But with the return of the cause she would have another violent, uncontrollable attack. One could not imagine cries more expressive of hopeless despair, or a more pathetic figure than this baby monkey looking from her cage to her relatives in the tree-tops and moaning wistfully.

But after almost a year of captivity Claudia's health deteriorated to the point that she no longer greeted Chapman and could barely drag herself to the play tree in her cage. Then, exactly one year after her capture, she died.

Chapman's final diary entry reads:

> Her body is in a jar of alcohol in the laboratory awaiting dissection to determine the cause of her death. I have never had the courage to examine it. Whatever the autopsy may show I believe that Claudia died of a broken heart.

It may be that future generations of howler monkeys will be found only in zoos or the cages of field research stations. In the vision that haunts me, these howlers will be running back and forth in their cages, looking for a proper stand of forest to call home. But there will be no towering cecropia, wild fig, or other such trees in sight. The encaged howlers, much like Claudia, will then start to roar uncontrollably, louder and louder, in the hope of attracting a friendly troop. But there will be none left to hear them.

I pray this vision never comes to pass.

WATCHING THE BIRDS, WATCHING THE WATCHERS

~

In May 1980 my wife Kathleen presented me with a trip to Florida as a kind of welcome-home celebration after I had spent long months at sea in a cold climate. She had made all the arrangements. All I had to do was agree to go.

The trip my wife had chosen was especially designed for bird-watching, an activity we both enjoy. It would have as its destination the low-lying islets and coral reefs 60 miles west of Key West, Florida, collectively known as the Dry Tortugas.

Scheduled to lead us was a world-renowned bird-guide author and artist, often called the dean of American ornithologists, aided by an author and naturalist well known for both his fiction and nonfiction. Among other attractions participants were guaranteed sightings of the sooty tern, an oceanic wanderer that gathers by the thousands at the Tortugas each spring for nesting, and the brown noddy, a ternlike bird, which also breeds there and is seldom seen anywhere else in the United States. Other species not often found except in our lower latitudes included the black noddy; the magnificent frigatebird; the blue-faced, or masked, booby; the red-footed booby; and perhaps even the elegant and lovely white-tailed tropicbird.

I could scarcely refuse, even though I had never before traveled on guided group tours and harbored a suspicion I would not like them. So it was that we put to sea on a ship—a ship in a manner of speaking—from Marathon Island in the Florida Keys on a fine spring day with stiff off-shore breezes. Our mode of conveyance was a large motor catamaran inappropriately named the *Happy Days*, as nearly as I can remember. Its normal function was to take 30 or 40 sport fishermen and an almost equal number of beer kegs for a weekend of bottom fishing for groupers, red snappers, sea bass, and other denizens of the Florida seafloor.

When we first went below to the *Happy Days*' main salon to put away our bags, we were treated to the first of many shocks the trip was to provide. To enter the salon was to be blinded by a sea of white—white sheets, that is—covering bunks stacked four high in long rows separated only by two narrow passageways.

"These here is your sleeping quarters," a young deckhand announced and then ran quickly out of sight.

At the forward end of this dormitory, as we preferred to call it, was a small door to starboard marked MEN. A door similarly situated on the port side announced an equal facility for WOMEN. Aft, or at the stern end of the salon, was a minuscule lunch counter with a faded sign that gave the price of such epicurean items as Texas-Style Chili, Kosher Franks, Burritos, and Whopper Burgers. Such was the total inventory, stem to stern, of the *Happy Days'* grand salon.

"I can't believe this!" my wife hissed in a loud whisper. "Go speak to the captain! There must be other arrangements."

As I debated whether or not to do her bidding, I saw that none of the other 30-odd passengers seemed disturbed or unhappy with the accommodations. Some of the older members of the group made jokes about how the sleeping quarters bore a strong resemblance to the bunk rooms of World War II troop transports. Others drew lots to see who would sleep in the bottom bunks, which required lying down on the deck flooring in order to crawl into them.

In this manner I quickly learned an important truth about bird-watchers. Simply stated, it is that they seldom complain about a lack of amenities or creature comforts. Birders, as they prefer to style themselves, will slog through malarial swamps, brave the chilling winds of the Arctic tundra, or camp out in rain forests rich in insect fauna, all without protest, as long as there are birds to see. Roughing it becomes a way of life to them, in fact, and to endure it, a kind of badge of honor.

"Be quiet," I therefore whispered to my wife, telling her that to get along with our fellow birders we would have to go along, as the common expression has it.

In short order the *Happy Days* rounded Marathon Key and put out to sea. Soon she was bucking the steep seas which always rear up when northwest winds meet the Gulf Stream's strong currents. Little by little, I happened to notice, some among our group were heading quietly to the far rail or seeking the questionable privacy of their dormitory bunks.

"Look, a Bonnie, off to the left!" a woman passenger stationed at the port rail shouted in exultation. Her friends ran to her, clamoring for more precise directions. A Bonnie, I subsequently learned, is a Bonaparte's gull. Although the Bonaparte's cannot truly be called a rare species, it is certainly not as abundant as many other gulls of the Atlantic littoral.

"Sorry," the same woman called out a moment later, much less loudly than before. "It's a laughing, after all."

A groan of disappointment now came from her friends. The laughing gull, the reader should know, is described in most bird guides as "a very common coastal species."

"Audubon's shearwater, off the port bow, ten o'clock,

about 70 yards," our author-naturalist now announced in authoritative tones.

A great wave of "ooh's" and "aah's!" rose from all those standing by the port rail. Those on the starboard side rushed to join them. Sure enough, there was a small and dark shearwater darting over the waves, now at least a hundred yards distant. The bird seemed to be flying hard on the wind, with very few of the spectacular swoops and glides of its larger relatives.

"Who hasn't got an Audubon?" someone now asked.

"I don't think Emily has one," a friend replied.

"Are you sure?" the first speaker now asked.

"I'm almost certain," was the reply. "I'll go down and ask her."

In due course Emily was roused out of her bunk and escorted topside, her face ashen and her step unsteady. Nothing daunted, she braced herself against the rail, swept the horizon with her binoculars, and soon found the Audubon's shearwater, now nothing more than a little speck above the horizon. She then scribbled some notes in a small black notebook and started back for her bunk. To my surprise her pale face was now aglow with an unmistakable smile of satisfaction.

"The Audubon's a life bird for Emily," the person next to me kindly explained. Emily had made a note of it because she could now enter the Audubon's shearwater in her life list, or the master record of every species a dedicated bird-watcher sees in his or her lifetime. When I asked my neighbor if Emily had really been able to observe the bird, at least well enough to identify it in the future, I was told this was not necessary. She had made a confirmed sighting, confirmed in this case by an expert, no less. She was therefore entitled to add it to her list. That was how it worked.

"Don't you have a life list?" my neighbor now asked me.

From this interchange I learned a second great truth about bird-watchers; namely, that for a great many birders nothing is more rewarding than adding a bird to one's life list. Even the worst case of *mal de mer* such as Emily obviously suffered will not stand in the way of such a prize. Charlton Ogburn in his splendid *The Adventure of Birds* writes of a frightful offshore trip aboard one of the deep-sea fishing charter boats, whose captains try to keep busy in winter with day trips for bird-watchers out of Ocean City, Maryland. The day was very cold and the seas rough enough so that some among the group became seasick immediately after passing through Ocean City's twin jetties. Others soon followed suit or injured themselves as the boat pounded some 40 or 50 miles out to sea. But once on the offshore grounds all the passengers were on their feet shouting with delight at frequent sightings of gannets, kittiwakes, and other pelagic seabirds for whom the open ocean is their true home. Only the alcids, or the family that includes auks, murres, and guillemots, seemed to be missing.

Of the return trip Ogburn has written:

> The deck of the cabin is covered with the bodies of the seasick and others are bent over and pale on the benches outside. . . . Those of us who have not sought refuge, and courted nausea, in the crowded infirmary of the heated cabin are huddled together in its lee, braced one way or another against the cavortings of the vessel, gloves soaked with spray, shoes with the water sloshing about on the deck.

But, Ogburn concludes, there was no question but that his fellow passengers "will oversubscribe the next charter trip in the hope of better weather and some of those refractory alcids."

As the afternoon shadows lengthened and the *Happy Days* surged ahead in diminishing winds, we made a strange and unusual landfall, unusual to me, at least, because I had never seen the like in many years of seagoing. An odd building, an odd brick-and-stonework building seemed to be emerging right out of the sea, shimmering and dancing on the sunlit waves of the far horizon. It appeared to be a factory, a large and low-lying factory with its ground floor in the water. Or was it a prison, as its harsh outlines and isolated location seemed to suggest?

The latter proved to be correct, our leaders soon told us. The building was in fact Fort Jefferson, originally built after the war of 1812 to guard the eastern approaches to our Gulf ports. For many years it had the distinction of being the largest brick structure in the United States. But after the outbreak of the Civil War, the fort was captured by Union forces and used as a prison that became a particular hell reserved for Union deserters, many of whom were chained to the walls of its damp dungeons.

Presently our full complement of passengers was on deck as we threaded our way through coral reefs and sandy islets, raising noisy clouds of the promised sooty terns and some brown noddies as well. Within minutes the *Happy Days* was tied up to a wooden pier leading to a drawbridge over the fort's moat. At the end of the drawbridge was a massive wooden portal framed by thin columns of granite. It was the fort's only entranceway, now kept permanently open.

Happy with their seabird sightings, our group members quickly trooped ashore and marched through the portal into what was euphemistically known as the parade ground, or a field of rough grass and small gumbo-limbo and buttonwood trees where prisoners were once mustered for work details and drills. The dean, as we took to calling our senior leader, told us a storm front had passed two days before and that the 12-acre parade ground might therefore be a welcome resting place for the many migrating warblers and other small land birds heading north across the Gulf of Mexico at this time of year. To be sure, soon there were exultant cries of "Look, a black-throated green!" or "Over here, a blackpoll and a yellow!"

I held back, however. The grim reality of the fort's presence—its sheer massiveness, its ruined battlements, and its extreme isolation—held me rooted to the spot. Just inside the entrance was a small dungeon chamber that served as the fort's temporary information center, unattended and equipped only with a push-button slide projector and a loose-leaf notebook. Here I learned that the chamber had once been the private cell of the unfortunate Dr. Samuel Mudd, the physician who answered a midnight call and treated the broken leg of a disguised John Wilkes Booth, President Lincoln's assassin; that the Dry Tortugas were first discovered during Ponce de León's futile quest for the elixir of eternal youth; and that the battleship U.S.S. *Maine* stopped at the fort's coaling docks for bunker in February 1898, just before making its next and last port of call in Havana, Cuba.

Nearby was a sign pointing to a narrow stone stairway leading to the fort's second tier, once its principal gun gallery. The sign urged visitors to exercise extreme caution while exploring the fort and warned of the dangers of loose bricks, dislodged stonework, and empty rain cisterns. Given such a challenging invitation, I quickly decided that a tour of the fort might prove more interesting than an hour or two of birding on the parade ground. I therefore cast a quick glance at our group, making sure no one could see me, and ran for the stairway.

Up on the second tier I found myself walking down a

long hallway of tall and narrow brickwork arches, which seemed to recede to a diminishing infinity, like the images formed by a room of mirrors in an amusement parks funhouse. There were 110 of these arches in all along the half-mile of the fort's interior perimeter; the cool and damp shade they cast was a welcome relief from the fierce glare of the late afternoon sun. My footsteps echoed as I walked under them, and there were strange hollow sounds when I scuffed pebbles or small stones into empty rain cisterns.

The third tier was by contrast open to the skies, open and unfinished, since it was abandoned during the construction period when it was discovered that the fort's great weight was causing it to sink in its coralline limestone foundations. But the view it offered was spectacular. All the coral reefs, small islands, and sandy shallows that constitute the Dry Tortugas were in plain sight. Far to the north I could see long white lines of surf breaking on coral reefs and, behind them, the opalescent blues and greens so often found in sheltered lagoon waters. To the west was Loggerhead Key, named after one of the three sea turtles that frequent the islands and gave them their Spanish name. The largest of the Tortugas islands, Loggerhead is the site of a lighthouse of the same name, a Coast Guard station, and a respectable stand of palm trees bordering an inviting white sand beach.

Closest at hand and by far the most noticeable both visually and audibly, however, was Bush Key, a half-mile sliver of sand, sea grasses, and bay cedar bushes directly east of the fort. Here each spring more than 100,000 sooty terns make their nests, which in reality are nothing more than shallow depressions in the sand. Incredibly, they share the small island at peak season with some 2,000 brown noddies, which prefer to nest in what little vegetation Bush Key has to offer. Almost equal numbers of birds seemed to be in the air, I soon discovered through my binoculars, since like many seabirds the males and females of both species take turns sitting on their nests. Now, as the evening sun sank to the horizon, mates were returning from their offshore foraging grounds in great numbers. I watched in fascination as long and ragged flight lines converged from every point in the compass into one great hovering mass above the islands. The noise from their calls was astounding. The sooty terns shrilled their *wideawake-wideawake,* as some bird guides choose to render their calls by onomatopoeia, and the brown noddies let forth with what has been variously transcribed as a guttural *kark-kark* or crowlike *kwok-kwok.* But tempting as it may be to make fun of some of these efforts at transcription, we must remember that they are a serious matter to the returning birds, since they serve as one of the primary homing devices—the close-range sonar, if you prefer—by which mated pairs find each other in crowded seabird colonies. Each of the thousands of *kark-kark*'s or *wideawake-wideawake*'s is an individual voice, as recognizable to its hearers as human voices are to us.

Returning in the near dark, I found the *Happy Days* waiting for me with all hands aboard and ready to cast off for a nighttime anchorage. I quickly joined a group on the foredeck and nodded my head or made appreciative comments as they discussed the various birds they had seen that afternoon. In this way I hoped that no one would notice much less bring up my defection. But my wife Kathleen soon joined the group. "Where were you?" she immediately asked rather loudly. "We thought you might have had an accident."

All through supper, mercifully provided from some freeze lockers of prepared dishes and not the hot-dog stand, various members of the group went over the day's list of the birds they had seen, sometimes engaging in lively discussions about which were fully confirmed sightings and which should be relegated to the category known as probables. Yellow-throated warbler, redstart, white-throated sparrow—the list went on. It was indeed a splendid start for the definitive list, as one of our leaders chose to call it, and I began to feel guilty for not having participated in it. This was, after all, a birding trip, not a tour of historical sites.

On deck after supper I joined another group who were eagerly comparing other birding trips they had taken. One among them, an overweight gentleman who carried a large spotting telescope and a camera with three different lenses, told me he was finding our trip satisfactory, but not to be compared with a flight to Alaska's Aleutian Islands he had made the summer before.

"Oh, yes," he said, "I got ten lifers in the Aleutians."

The ten lifers, as I suspected, meant ten new life birds. That was why he had gone to the Aleutians in the first place, he said, to add more birds to his life list. Not only that, he had gotten good photographs of most of them.

"That's nothing, a lady replied. "My friend Mimi got 20 up there."

"Well, anyhow, I'm over the 800 mark," the overweight gentleman answered in a voice that swelled with satisfaction.

From subsequent conversations I learned that the Aleutian Islands—the distant Aleutians like Attu and Kiska, that is, which extend almost to the Siberian mainland—were fast becoming a popular destination for hardcore birders. In fact, difficult and expensive though the trip might be, the western Aleutians were almost de rigueur for birders who wanted to pass the 800-species benchmark for North America. Not long ago the goal of most American birders was to spot 600 species, or the approximate number known to breed in North America north of Mexico. But in more recent years the American Birding Association has decreed that birds that regularly migrate to our continent, as well as casual, vagrant, and even accidental visitors, may also be counted, though none of them may breed in North America. Given this expanded definition, the Aleutians offer many rare and wonderfully adorned seabirds, such as the whiskered auklet or the tufted puffin, as well as many migrants and casual visitors from the Asian mainland, such as the long-toed stint or the Siberian rubythroat. More than enough, in other words, to boost the diligent life lister over the prized 800 mark. This, I inferred from the group's conversation, conferred instant status on all who passed it.

Back in the dormitory the overhead lights had been switched off and replaced by small night-lights. Even so, some among the group were still discussing their personal lists or arguing about "probables" versus "confirmeds." From my bunk at the cabin-floor level I looked far down an aisle and saw that the dean was having a difficult time climbing up to his top-row bunk. "Come on, hon', you can do it!" his younger wife urged. She then braced herself and gave him a helpful push, which happily boosted him over the top.

Soon there were no more sounds except for a few staccato snores and the gentle lap of waves against the *Happy Days'* waterline.

The next morning I vowed to stay with the group and be a good birder. Our leaders suggested a return to the parade ground, since new waves of migrants might be expected overnight. We started off in good fashion, finding not only warblers but also sparrows, veeries, some thrushes, and a lone grosbeak. But after less than an hour the dean spotted a falcon circling high overhead. As the bird came lower and closer, he identified it positively as a merlin.

The group responded, myself included, with what was almost a shout of excitement. There it was, one of the rarest of falcons, circling above us in the blue ceiling of the sky, riding the first morning thermals rising from the fort. After gaining sufficient height the bird swooped low in a shallow arc above the parade ground. This process was repeated three or four times as the falcon searched for some form of feathered prey, or so I imagined.

Each of the bird's passes provoked new expressions of admiration from all of us. But in time the group moved on across the grounds. There were, of course, many more migrant species to be added to the trip's list. I hung back, however, and positioned myself comfortably in the shade of a low gumbo-limbo tree. As one who has passed long moments simply tracing the flight of more common raptors, I was determined not to let the merlin out of sight for as long as it chose to remain over Fort Jefferson.

Then it happened. Instead of one more pass of inspection the merlin partially tucked its wings and began a steep dive that seemed to be aimed right in my direction. So fast was the dive—100 to 200 miles an hour is the accepted norm—that I could not follow it with my binoculars. Instinctively, I ducked.

Within a split second there was a soft sound—a sort of audible puff is the only way I can describe it—which seemed close to my left ear. I turned in that direction.

There was nothing to see but a small grayish white feather floating slowly in the air. Quickly I raised my binoculars and caught sight of the fast-receding merlin. In its clasped feet was a small bird, no larger than a warbler. The merlin seemed to be cradling it, or shifting it around within its talons for a more secure grasp. In this manner I watched it disappear beyond the fort, out over the sea.

All things considered, it had been a rare and spectacular event. I found it hard to imagine how a falcon's eye can pick out such tiny targets as warblers or other small songbirds from a height of 400 or 500 feet, much less set a proper course to intercept them. Then, even as the bird rockets down in its vertiginous dive, it must make constant flight corrections, constant minute shifts to correspond with the darting and erratic flight of such small targets, and at the last split second, arrest its power dive and bring forward its talons. It is truly a virtuoso feat of sight, speed, and aerobatics.

When I finally looked around me again, our group was nowhere to be seen. How could this be, I wondered, not without rising concern. One more defection and I would surely be ostracized by the group. Perhaps the leaders had opted for a brief tour of the fort. I therefore ran over to the Information Center and up the crumbling stairway as fast as possible to the third tier.

There was no trace of my fellow passengers. But what I did find brought joy to my heart. Above me calmly riding the updrafts on the windward side of the fort was a flight of magnificent frigatebirds, a seabird I love to watch. They seemed to be hanging almost motionless in the air, so close above me that one bird periodically cocked its head to look me over with such intensity that I began to wonder who was really watching whom. Other birds silently changed places, with only minute or imperceptible movements of their long and narrow wings. Still others, seemingly having nothing better to do, scratched their heads with one of their small feet or relieved themselves with surprising force. Occasionally one of the other birds might swoop down to pluck small fish from the surface of the sea with their long and wickedly hooked bills; or more rarely, fly off in pursuit of a tern that had just caught a fish, harassing it until it dropped or disgorged its prey for the frigatebird to catch in midair.

In this manner the magnificents pass their airborne hours, soaring effortlessly and constantly scanning the sea. As I watched them, I began to think how in fact they have no other choice. So adapted are they to aerial existence that they can neither walk on land nor dive or swim in water. They must keep to the air, or else. And the only else, the only alternative, is a secure roosting-place perch in a seaside tree or high bush.

But soon one lone bird began an unusual activity I had seen only once before. First it soared in lazy circles to a point well above all the other frigatebirds. Having thus gained a considerable height, it went into a steep power dive during which its partly folded wings shivered and trembled to such a degree that it looked as though the bird's whole body was shaking. Then, just like a dive-bomber putting on the brakes, it pulled out sharply from its dive and started circling upward again. It repeated this maneuver not once but many times. I remembered that on the first occasion I had seen it on the Pacific coast of Guatemala, I had thought that since the magnificents cannot enjoy dust baths on land or bathing in water, all the shivering and shaking might be an air bath, so to speak, in which microscopic parasites went the way of the wind. Now, with this second sighting, I began to think the maneuver was a courtship display. After all, many other birds perform their courtship by aerial acrobatics. The bird in question was also obviously a male, easily distinguished by its red gular patch, which it normally blows up like two red balloons for a very showy courtship signal. But this bird showed no sign of making such a display. Moreover, not one of the female birds was paying him the slightest attention. Perhaps lonely and unrequited males behave this way, going through the motions by force of habit long after any opportunity for attracting a partner has passed.

Soon my exercise in empirical reasoning was rudely cut short by a distant blast from a ship's horn. I turned to see the *Happy Days* approaching a dock at Loggerhead Key more than two miles distant. Once again I had managed to be left behind! Now I would certainly be the pariah of the group, to say nothing of the fact that I dearly wanted a refreshing swim and something to eat. Dejectedly I climbed down to the parade ground and walked out to the pier beyond the drawbridge. As luck would have it, however, the fort's lone Park Service ranger happened to be there, and he soon asked if I didn't "belong with the others." Mercifully, he took me aboard his outboard skiff and soon we were skimming along making good speed for Loggerhead Key. Once there I thanked him profusely for his help and stepped ashore to find the group widely scattered on the island's western shore. Some were happily lounging on its fine white-sand beach, others snorkeled along its fringing coral reef, and still others doggedly tramped inland through the island's undergrowth in search of new species to add to their life lists. It came to me first as a surprise and then, I must confess, as something of a disappointment that no one seemed to have noticed my absence. Except, of course, my wife.

"Where were you this time?" she asked in a rather matter-of-fact manner.

After a pleasant afternoon at Loggerhead Key and a cool anchorage for the night, the *Happy Days* set course for Marathon the next morning. For the return voyage the captain elected to use the more sheltered route north of the isolated mangrove cays and underwater reefs that run east-west to Key West, rather than outside them on the still boisterous Gulf Stream. Some among those who did not get seasick were disappointed with this decision, since they had hoped to find more offshore species to add to their trip or life lists.

But for the most part the *Happy Days* returned with a cheerful complement of passengers who were relieved to be on calmer waters and more than satisfied with the trip as a whole. Many of them had added significantly to their life lists. Others were still trying to do so with discussions of probables versus confirmeds, now in a more amicable or helpful manner. Then, too, there was the trip list, which was also something to celebrate. It already topped 110 species, the dean told us, which was more birds than any previous trip to the Dry Tortugas had recorded. Among them were all the promised tropical species, even the lovely white-tailed tropicbirds.

By comparison my trip list was minuscule. And I cannot deny that I secretly wished I had seen the tropicbirds and a number of other species that were on nearly everyone else's lists. But there were other considerations. There was the image of the swarming thousands of sooty terns, for example, bringing order out of seeming chaos as they sought out their individual nest mates. Or the pinpoint accuracy of the merlin's swoop and the effortless flight of the frigate-birds. These were all experiences that gave me fresh appreciations of the world of birds, images I have not forgotten. By contrast I think my wife Kathleen, enthusiastic birder though she may be, would now have great difficulty in recalling any five or six species seen on the Dry Tortugas trip. The same could well be true of many of the *Happy Days* passengers, those who seldom forget what species they have seen in their lifetimes but are often at a loss to tell the time, place, and circumstance of their viewings.

It is true that over the years since the *Happy Days* cruise I have become a wiser and much more enthusiastic birder. At my wife's urging I have even taken another guided group tour in which, as luck would have it, all the other members were eight women, eight highly competitive women, that is, of the kind that the genial seabird expert Peter Harrison calls CB's, or Combat Birders. And I have also led one tour—and only one for reasons that will soon be apparent—featuring shorebirds at Virginia's Chincoteague National Wildlife Refuge.

One aspect of my bird-watching which has not changed, however, is the slow and deliberate pace of my observations. This means that I continue to miss the boat, both figuratively and literally speaking, as when a bus tour operator left me stranded high on a cloud-forested mountain in Costa Rica named, quite appropriately as I thought at the time, Cerro de la Muerte. (Yes, my fellow birders eventually counted heads and kindly asked the driver to return for me.) Or the time I lost the shorebird tour group I was leading for the Smithsonian Associates, I am ashamed to admit, all because I wandered off to watch a great egret struggling to ingest a large water snake for the better part of a half-hour. But these are embarrassments I am fated to endure since I continue to believe that the most rewarding kind of bird-watching requires time—time "to keep under attentive view or observation, as in order to learn something," which happens to be one of the primary definitions of the verb "to watch" in my dictionary.

It is also true that over the years I have come around to a grudging respect—even admiration or awe, in some cases—for my life-lister friends. This has come with the gradual realization that no branch of the natural sciences has benefitted more from the contributions of amateurs than ornithology—veritable armies of dedicated amateurs, I should say—numbering many millions according to recent surveys by the Bureau of Census and the U.S. Fish and Wildlife Service. (These surveys have shown that 63.1 million Americans have wild-bird feeders at their homes and that 24.7 million adults take at least one trip a year specifically to watch birds, spending more than $14 billion a year on necessary equipment, travel expenses, and membership in birding associations.) Among the contributions they make, to cite one example, are the well-known Christmas counts which many Audubon societies sponsor across the nation. In these counts competent birders fan out in broad sectors from their home grounds to note and list the numbers of every species they can identify from dawn to dusk. Since some Audubon societies have been conducting

Christmas counts for over a century, the long-term records they can provide are a boon to scientists studying the dynamics of bird populations and their winter ranges. Other societies and organizations conduct counts seasonally throughout the year, as for example, the Annual Bloomin' Birdathon Tally Rally, which my local society exuberantly launches every June. These counts further define ranges and can be invaluable in determining breeding grounds as well as species populations.

The contribution is international, moreover, because a number of European countries now have their armies of dedicated watchers. This is especially true of England, which I would guess has more ardent watchers proportion-ate to its population than the United States. Witness the annual invasion of the Scilly Isles off Land's End; it is said that British bird-watchers by the hundreds descend on the Scillies during spring and fall migrations, when even North American species blown off course may fetch up for a rest, to say nothing of a number of local rarities.

Still, American bird-watchers may well be the ultimate internationalists. There is no corner of the world to which American birding tours have not gone. They have traveled from the mountain jungles of New Guinea to the glaciers and snowfields of Spitsbergen, from Central America to Panama, a particularly special area of concen-tration where well-trained guides and experienced partic-ipants have mapped out the ranges of North American migrants as well as the rich tropical avifaunas.

So it is. I continue to respect those who keep careful lists and thus help the serious study of birds. But I will shy away from any more tours, partly because of a fear I may again be thrown in with Combat Birders and partly because I continue to believe the solitary way of seeing birds is the most enriching. To put it another way, I believe the slow pace of "keep[ing] under attentive view or observation, as in order to learn something" has its own rewards.

As I write these lines in my home in Washington, D.C., in the month of January, a pair of evening grosbeaks has flown into the woods behind our house. A moderate winter wind is blowing and fine powder snow sifts gently off tree branches. Beneath them the grosbeaks are industriously pecking under the snow, making their way to the spillage of seeds at the base of our feeding station. Their rich yellow-and-black bodies stand out brilliantly, adding a cheerful note to the winter landscape. But what interests me most is the novelty of their appearance, since it has been some time—how long I cannot tell—since we have seen them on our home grounds. Does this signal a decline? Or is it a natural wintertime variance, as bird guides suggest?

Perhaps I should stop now and record this event, noting carefully the time and place. And then I might do the same with other unusual or interesting sightings, especially spring arrivals and fall departures. It wouldn't really be a life list, you understand, just a file system for periodic observations. Properly maintained, it might help me to understand a number of questions. For example, what *is* happening to the evening grosbeaks?

WITH A
LITTLE HELP
~

In the mid-1960s young Americans took to the woods and climbed mountains as never before. Fueling this new generation of *Wandervogel* were such disparate elements as political dissent, heightened awareness of the environment, and books such as Euell Gibbons's *Stalking the Wild Asparagus* and Colin Fletcher's *The Thousand Mile Summer*. The "greening of America," in short, became the catch-phrase of the day.

Almost as important as any of the above was a vast array of new equipment that made extended hiking trips in the wilderness both easier and safer. The key item—better said, the foundation, literally and figuratively—was the tubular-frame backpack. Unlike the ungainly rucksacks hikers had long suffered, the aluminum-frame pack distributed weight more evenly over most of the upper torso, thus permitting heavier loads and easier walking with a more correct posture. There were also such innovations as small white-gas stoves, freeze-dried foods, lightweight pup tents, and air or foam mattresses, to mention a few.

Eventually, as might be expected, both the spirit of the greening and the lure of the new equipment reached some among the middle-aged. In my case, I am sure, it was more the latter. To be more specific, it began the moment I found Colin Fletcher's *The Complete Walker* in a bookstore in the early 1970s, by which time the book had gone through 13 printings and gained best-seller status. What first caught my eye was a full-color photograph on the dust jacket of over one hundred "essentials" for extended hiking trips—tent, sleeping bag, plastic canteens and food containers, aluminum ware, freeze-dried foods and drinks, extra boots, slippers, medicines, pillboxes, and much, much more—all neatly laid out on a white sheet, spread out on what looked like a well-manicured green lawn. Without further thought, I bought the book, took it home, and began to devour its contents.

The next step logically enough was to find one of the new-generation outdoor-equipment stores. Unfortunately, in the city where I live, there was but one such at the time, far out in the suburbs. Choices, therefore, were limited. This was especially true of the key item, or the frame pack that

Colin Fletcher called "the house on your back." The pack that fit me best was decidedly unorthodox. Instead of one large bag with perhaps one or two interior dividing spaces and some outside flap pockets, it had four horizontal compartments, each with its own zipper opening. These compartments, moreover, were colored a garish red, white, and blue, so distinctly, in fact, that I first spotted the pack from far across the sales room.

"Would you happen to have this model in a plain color?" I asked.

No, that was not possible, the salesman claimed. He thought the company that manufactured it didn't carry the model anymore. It was a shame, he thought, because color-coded compartments were a big help, a memory aid for organizing and finding items when on the trail. Then there was the safety factor. "Suppose you take a tumble into a gully," he added. "You're lying there, stunned, facedown in the leaves and dirt, in a forest-green pack. So who's going to see you?"

I came home not only with the multicolored backpack but also a pup tent, a Swedish white-gas stove, a Sierra Club stainless-steel cup with a wire handle that could double as a mini-cooking pot, first-aid and snake-bite kits, two kinds of bug repellent, high-energy snack bars, and many other such oddments. Suffice it to say that outdoor-equipment stores are the greatest inducement to compulsive buying since the advent of supermarkets.

"Where exactly are you going with all that?" my oldest daughter asked in a voice that betrayed deep suspicion. "Does all this have anything to do with our plans for next summer?"

"Hey, guys, look at Pops and his Yankee Doodle bag!" my son announced to his siblings the moment I tried on the pack frame.

Where exactly to go with all my new gear was no problem. My thoughts immediately turned to northern Maine, or more specifically the area around Mount Katahdin, Maine's highest peak and the northern terminus of the Appalachian National Scenic Trail. I had previously enjoyed brief visits with a friend who had the only camp on the eastern shore of the string bean-shaped Chesuncook Lake, one of Maine's longest, from which Henry David Thoreau and his Indian guide Joe Polis first "had a view of the mountains about Ktaadin . . . apparently twenty-five or thirty miles distant, their summits concealed by clouds." At the time of my first visit it was the last year of lumberjacks and logging river drives. I remember being much impressed by a powerful little tugboat chugging down Chesuncook's 20-mile length, towing huge floating booms of four-foot logs to the south end of the lake. There they were unceremoniously shoved over a 140-foot dam to bob down the rapids of the West Branch of the Penobscot River to the giant paper mills of Millinocket. I was also equally or more impressed by the long sweep of the Maine woods which can be viewed along certain approaches to Mount Katahdin. At 5,286 feet, Katahdin is not New England's highest peak, but nowhere in the East does a mountain so dominate the surrounding land. Not only from Chesuncook but at various other vantage points, it can be seen from a great distance over an undulating plain of green. Nowhere else in my experience is there such a commanding view of the Maine woods. Nor, for some, a stronger inducement to explore them.

Yes, I thought, I would hike far into those woods somewhere in the shadow of Katahdin to prove my mettle as a backpacker. Not incidentally, I would also look over a lodge where my wife and I hoped to take our six children as a change from our annual excursions to the Maine coast. (My eldest daughter's intuitions, as usual, were uncannily correct.) After studying all 64 pages of the Appalachian Mountain Club's publication devoted to the Katahdin area, the *A.M.C. Maine Mountain Guide*, my thoughts turned to the Russell Pond campground. "This campground is a convenient and interesting hiking base," the guide intoned. "The wildlife in this remote area is especially intriguing." There were also new lean-tos and prepared tent sites, and the distance from the jumping-off spot at Roaring Brook was cryptically noted as "7 m. (3 hrs. 45 min.)." All these factors were well suited to what I had in mind. Without question Russell Pond was the ideal destination. There followed another period of compulsive buying, this time for nearly every book in print about the Maine woods and a shcaf of U.S. Geological Survey quad maps encompassing most of the northern part of the state.

As for timing, there was no question. I would start in mid-June, when I planned to take a self-declared sabbatical from my duties as one of the Smithsonian Institution's assistant secretaries in order to have time to write for myself. Previous experience with attempting to write books or even magazine articles at night and on weekends had come to almost nothing. Time off was essential. I would make a clean break from my Smithsonian duties by getting out of town, well beyond the reach of telephones. What exactly to write could be decided later. Like Henry David Thoreau I would first have a refreshing period of contemplation in the Maine woods and then come home to a *furor scribendi*.

So it came about that on a bright morning in mid-June I caught an early flight to Bangor, Maine, and rented a car to drive some hundred-odd miles north to Baxter State Park, within which lay both Mount Katahdin and Russell Pond. Along the way there were glimpses of log jams in the West Branch of the Penobscot and tantalizing views of Katahdin's summit.

Arriving at the Baxter State Park I cheerfully announced my intentions to the ranger on duty at the park's gatehouse. Much to my astonishment he told me I could not camp at Russell Pond. All the places were taken, he said.

"No problem," I answered, pointing to my Yankee Doodle

bag, thinking he referred to the lean-tos and prepared tent sites. "I have my own tent and air mattress."

"Sir, you don't understand," the ranger answered. "We only allow so many campers per night in Baxter, and there's no room at Russell."

I told him I thought the park policy was admirable. I quite understood, but surely he wouldn't turn away someone who had come all the way from Washington, D.C., who truly respected the environment, and who, as a matter of fact, looked forward to coming back to the Katahdin area with his wife and children later in the summer.

"Sir, you don't understand," the ranger repeated. "People write in for reservations in the winter, five or six months in advance. We can't go making exceptions."

I stood there, overcome by dashed hopes and a sense of defeat.

"You might want to check back here after twelve noon tomorrow," he added. "There might be some cancellations."

I camped for the night at a lake outside the park in a designated area shared by a trailer with license plates from nearby New Hampshire. The owner told me that he, too, was very disappointed, since Baxter policy did not allow auto or truck campers to spend the night. They could drive through the park's narrow roads and stop for lunch or whatever at certain selected places. But that was it. "Big deal," he said, somewhat sourly.

Trying to put the best face on things, I reasoned that it was probably a good idea to be trying out my tent and all my other essentials close to civilization. It wouldn't do to be surprised in the wild or have any gear failures "in a remote area with intriguing wildlife," in the words of the AMC guide.

Proving the point, it took me over a half-hour to erect my lightweight tent complete with its fly sheet. Then I found I could not light my mini-stove. As I tinkered with it, a swarm of mosquitoes found me.

At this point the wife of the New Hampshire man appeared and invited me to have supper with them inside their trailer. "No use staying out there fighting all those 'skeeters," she said.

I, the solo backpacker who would brave the Maine woods, I the outdoorsman who shunned trailers and all such recreational motor vehicles, gladly and gratefully accepted the invitation.

The next morning, the trailer having left, I successfully lit the white-gas stove, prepared a hearty breakfast centered around powdered eggs, and went over my equipment list and trail maps probably for the tenth time in as many days. Shortly before noon I was on my way to the park gatehouse.

A pleasant-looking high school girl was on duty. No there had been no cancellations or no-shows, she reported with a smile.

After a moment of stunned silence, I took a deep breath and recited the now familiar litany of sorrows I had given the ranger the day before. There was the long flight from Washington, the drive from Bangor in a rental car, all the study and preparations I had made, all the new equipment I was so eager to try out, and, of course, my elaborate plans for returning to Baxter later in the summer with my wife and children.

The high-school girl clucked with sympathy, as though she fully understood my difficult situation, and then asked me how many children I had.

"Oh, yes!" I answered, eager to keep our conversation going for whatever reason. "I have two sons and four daughters. The sons are the oldest and the youngest, the four girls are in between. We expect to stay at the Kidney Pond camps and explore the park from there. I know some of them look forward to climbing Katahdin—"

The young lady broke in to say there was one slight possibility. She then excused herself and had a brief conversation on the gatehouse radio phone. I tried to eavesdrop but could not make out anything of significance.

"We don't normally tell people about this," she returned to say, this time with a broader smile, "but we have a camping place on a little island on Lake Wassataquoik. We keep a canoe hidden in the bushes on shore. It's just a short paddle."

I said that sounded very nice indeed. But where exactly

was this Lake Wassataquoik?

"Rhymes with what's-that-to-cook," she corrected me. "It's about two or three miles beyond Russell Pond."

Makes nine or ten, I immediately thought to myself, when you add on the seven miles to Russell Pond of the infallible AMC guide. Could I really do this on what I knew would be up-and-down terrain? Not only that, it was already afternoon.

"It's really a super place," the high-school girl added. "There are high mountains all around the lake, there's a 200-foot waterfall, and you can dive right into the water from some rocks at one end of the island."

"You can do it," she continued, perhaps sensing my doubts. "I went there myself earlier this month."

As anyone knowledgeable in the perversities of the male ego will know, this last bit of intelligence quickly became a challenge. Yes, of course, I would go, thank you very much.

The young lady again got on the radio telephone to the ranger station at Russell Pond. "OK, Barry, I've got a party of one, name of Warner," she said. "Sending him into you at 13-0-5. Over and out."

"Roger, wilco," the ranger answered. "We will be on the lookout. Tell him to check in with us. Over."

Committed! I thanked the young lady profusely and drove the park road to the Roaring Brook campground, where many trails begin, including various routes to the summit of Katahdin, at least one of which is technically difficult. I noticed a couple wearing knickers and cable-stitch stockings, loaded down with nylon ropes and climbing gear. It seemed to me that they gave me and my flashy Yankee Doodle bag an arch look, which I returned.

At the trailhead a young ranger asked about my destination and then started to recite a checklist of essential items for overnight stays in the park. When I produced just such a list I had previously made from my shirt pocket, he seemed very pleased. "Most famous climbers always do make lists," he told me.

Climbers? Why would he mistake me for a climber, I wondered. Or were there some significant elevations on my route that I had somehow not seen on my topographic maps?

With such troubling thoughts I shouldered my pack and had a last-minute debate about taking along my fly rod. The rod, or better said its plastic case, was much too long to strap to the pack frame. One way or another it was bound to catch on branches or other snags. But I knew most cold Maine lakes held nice little brook trout, and my passion for fly fishing overcame any such objections. I would simply carry the rod and its case by hand. Period.

The first 200 yards of the trail were quite steep, enough so to leave me panting and wondering whether my 40-pound pack was too much for a person of 130 pounds. But immediately thereafter the trail wound down through tall pines and an occasional stand of birch. The descent was easy on firm and dry ground, and the pungent but pleasing smell of pine sap was everywhere in the air. With it came the sense of wonder and anticipation I always experience when first entering the hidden world of forests.

But not for long. Very soon I came to Roaring Brook. Although probably little more than a trickle in dry times, it was now living up to its name with the freshets of spring. To my surprise I could not find any aids for crossing it, not even a stray log placed across the current by some considerate hiker. Rock hopping was required and I failed miserably, plunging one foot into the water and narrowly avoiding a fall by a desperate stab of the fly rod case. Furthermore, the trail thereafter became quite soggy and studded with rocks and tree roots. Then came more brooks as well. Although not the size or volume of Roaring, they were many in number. The trail was now following the lowest slopes along the eastern flanks of Mount Katahdin, and I imagined these little brooks came from the melting snow of shaded valleys and cirques high up on the mountain. Whatever their source they never allowed my shoes to dry. I nevertheless plodded on, every step marked by squishing sounds.

As the reader has now probably determined, all my careful preparations and buying sprees had overlooked two key items. First and foremost was a proper pair of hiking shoes. The pebble-grained walking shoes I was wearing had served me well on my home grounds, or the relatively easy footing of the Maryland section of the Appalachian Trail or the various trails of Virginia's Shenandoah National Park. But carrying a heavy pack on rough and rocky trails was quite another matter. As Colin Fletcher's *Complete Walker* puts it in the very first sentence of the equipment chapter, "The foundations of the house on your back are your feet and their footwear, and the cornerstone is a good pair of BOOTS."

The second item, I realized soon enough was a hiking staff. As Fletcher has written, a staff "turns . . . [the] heavily laden from an insecure biped into a confident triped." It is, as so many others have observed, the quintessential third leg.

I walked on, therefore, somewhat insecurely, trying occasionally to use the plastic fly rod case as a staff and bouncing on one foot or another in a foolish effort to squeeze moisture out of my socks. Presently a small stream came in to the right of the trail. The gentle sound of gurgling waters and a faint breeze sifting through the pines caused me to stop. I squirmed out of my pack, unzipped the top compartment, and extracted a repulsive-looking compressed meat bar; a "high energy mix" of dried fruits, nuts, and little green candy balls trademarked Gorp; and my Sierra Club drinking cup. (At the time giardia had not yet made its unfortunate appearance in the nation's waterways.) As I did so I became acutely aware of some insect bites on my face and arms. A few blackflies, the scourge of the Maine woods, had been following me as I walked. Now a small cloud hovered over me, with individuals constantly darting in and out for quick, sharp bites. The icy stream water, however, seemed the best I had ever tasted and even the repulsive meat bar was palatable. But a look at my U.S.G.S. quad map and some pages I had cut out of the AMC guide showed I had gone only a little more than three miles in two hours. It was necessary to push on.

The trail now seemed more benign and there were occasional clearings where one could glimpse the great peaks north of Katahdin, framed by a clear blue sky and racing clouds. Soon the woods closed in again and an enormous overhanging boulder, surely a glacial erratic, blocked the right half of the trail. I stepped warily around to its back side, where a black bear family might easily have hidden, but found nothing but cool shade and another attack by the omnipresent blackflies. I wanted to drink more stream water, but the very thought of unharnessing the pack and then struggling to put it back on dissuaded me, not to mention the fact that the AMC guide claimed the overhanging rock was only about half the distance to Russell Pond. I had to make better time. There was nothing for it but to plod on, although I now felt a pain in the ball of my left foot.

About an hour later there came a pleasing descent through a grove of native spruce followed by a clearing from which it was possible to see Russell Mountain, Katahdin's

nearest neighbor to the north. Inspiring as the view may
have been, I took greater joy in the fact that both my quad
maps and the guide suggested that there was no more than
a mile and a quarter to go to Russell Pond. I would make it
in good time after all and probably reach Lake Whatever-
Its-Name before dark.

But as had happened before, each time the trail passed
through easy terrain or presented pleasing views, serious
obstacles soon followed. This time it was the main branch
of the Wassataquoik Stream and a "two-log and three-wire
bridge" that spanned its churning rapids. These bridges are
so described because they consist of two logs driven into
the ground in the form of an X on both sides of the stream;
one heavy wire on which to slide your feet runs from the
crotch of one X to the other and the other two wires for
handholds run from the tops of each X. Needless to say,
caution and a good sense of balance are required for suc-
cessful crossings. But, still elated from the signs of my
progress, I bounded up the wooden access ladder thought-
fully provided by the park rangers and took two big steps
out on the lower wire. Panic immediately seized me. The
wires now danced and swayed back and forth in a wild sara-
bande, and as a result, I looked like one of those high-wire
circus performers trying to recover balance after a badly
executed stunt. Trying to regain my composure, I refused to
look down at the boiling rapids five or six feet below and
talked to myself. A fall won't kill you, I kept saying, but at

the same time I knew perfectly well that there would be injuries enough to put a quick end to my sylvan idyll.

With these conflicting thoughts I inched backward to the starting point. Sitting on the ladder steps, visibly shaken, I unhitched my pack, took a drink of stream water, and reached into my pocket for a cigarette. (Shocked readers should remember that at this time, the United States was by and large a smoking society, which included the outdoors and nature lovers as well.) I found none. Panic seized me again, as any former addict will understand, when I realized I had left two packs in the glove compartment of the rental car.

This new worry in mind, I successfully crossed the log-and-wire bridge by sliding my feet slowly and carefully all the way. Soon thereafter the welcome sight of the ranger station and its ample screened porch came into view. The friendly reception I received from the two rangers and the bug-free rest on their porch was the most welcome interlude of the day. Both rangers told me I had come at the height of the blackfly season. The younger of the two said that if campers had any sense they would stay out of the Maine woods at this time of year. I have been puzzling over the intent of that remark ever since, but at the time I was too happy, drinking cool well water and eating more Gorp in the shade of the porch to give it much thought. What is more, the older ranger, the Barry who answered the call from the gatehouse, was a smoker. Not only that, he favored my brand. After I offered him half of my best trout flies as an exchange, he kindly parted with a pack at cost.

I set off in high spirits for the remaining three miles. But any feeling of ebullience quickly vanished when I blundered into a quiet pond with mirror-black water. A quick look at the quad map showed it to be the aptly named Turner Deadwater. Not only that, I had gotten off to a bad start. Retracing my steps I eventually found some faint blue blazes that marked the trail to Lake What's-That-to-Cook. Shortly thereafter came more dead water, or, to be more precise, a swamp that was impossible to cross without wading calf-deep. As before, my every subsequent step was now marked by squishing sounds, not to mention black mud oozing out of my once fine pebble-grained walking shoes. Cursing, I vowed to pay closer attention to the trail blazes, since I now had a stronger feeling of being absolutely on my own. Ahead was only the wilder northern section of Baxter State Park, devoid of ranger stations or frequently traveled trails.

The trail now passed over a slight incline and then down into an area known as the Six Ponds, passing very closely between two of them. Square in the middle of the first pond to the left of the trail was a large bull moose standing shoulder-high in the water; in the pond to the right were two females doing the same. From time to time the big bull plunged his head and massive horns below the surface, exposing a powerful ridge of muscles between his shoulders. Then up again he would come, first the broad rack of his horns and then his equine-looking head. It was impossible not to envy the moose standing there in the cool water, free of all blackflies and at the same time obviously enjoying the aquatic plants that were his favored seasonal food. It was a picture-perfect scene—one often the subject of Maine postcards, in fact—and I wanted to stay there to savor it. But it was already after seven in the evening and there was more trail to hike and a camp to set up before dark.

At the next rise I stumbled on some matted willow bushes by the side of the trail, causing the topmost bar of the pack frame to give me a nasty rap on the back of my head. But whatever hurt I suffered vanished at the top of the rise. There below me was Lake What's-That-to-Cook! There, too, was the little island and there was the canoe, not hard to find, nestled in the bushes of the near shore.

I paddled the short distance to the island, perhaps no more than 40 yards, beached the canoe securely, and climbed up to the island's low crown. Here it was possible to stretch out on a soft carpet of pine needles and not be bothered by blackflies, thanks to a lake breeze that momentarily kept them at bay. I drank stream water from my plastic canteen, smoked the first of my cigarettes, and watched happily as a pair of loons periodically dove underwater and then bobbed up again, cautiously distancing themselves from me. It was a precious moment, one that I dearly wanted to prolong. But daylight was waning. There was yet that tent to set up and a meal to prepare.

Thanks to my practice run of the night before, the tent went up quite easily and the white-gas stove lit on the first try. No sooner had I finished, however, than a young bull moose with stubby horns in velvet started to wade across to the island from the opposite shore. He seemed to be heading right for the little area of higher ground where I had made camp, which seemed to me much too small a space to share. I therefore banged a spoon on my best cooking pot. The moose retreated.

What followed on that first night at Lake What's-That-to-Cook is perhaps best summarized by the shorthand notes of a running diary, which for reasons the reader will soon understand helped me to while away much of the following day. The first entries read:

9:00 p.m. Mini-stove roaring away in the gloaming. Great convenience. Moose starts out for island again. Blink flashlight right at him. Back to mainland he goes again. (Is this the right thing to do? Possibly I am interfering with his diurnal rounds?) Dine on Mountain House freeze-dried Beef 'N' Rice with Onions (damn good), half English muffin (untoasted) with marmalade, dates, two cookies, tea. Blackflies disappearing; mosquitoes taking their place.

10:15 p.m. Bugs force me into tent.

10:30 p.m. Out again to finish cleanup and inflate air mattress. Rest. Slide mattress into tent. Rest. Terrible racket in the woods. Two bobcats fighting unto death? Maybe just raccoons, though.

11:00 p.m. Into sleeping bag, finally. Some mosquitoes have crawled in with me, it seems. Try to sleep. I have a feeling that young moose is back on island. Worried by thoughts of him smashing right through my frail three-pound tent. And that screeching! Could well have been bobcats, or even Canada lynx.

11:30 p.m. Turn from back to side; draw up legs as much as my bag allows. MONSTER SEIZURE in left thigh! Worst cramp I have ever experienced. Sweat. Worry. Massage and fibrillate muscles. Pain eventually disappears. Try to sleep again. Assailed by thought what the hell is a 52-year-old man doing alone on island in Maine lake, 10 miles from nearest road and maybe 3 miles from nearest camper? Have stone bruise on ball of left foot, too. Still some mosquitoes in this damn tent.

12:15 a.m. Take Valium, 5 mg.

The next day, poor as my night's sleep may have been, I was invigorated by a cool and clear morning and the placid beauty of Lake Wassataquoik, for here let us give it the dignity of its proper Algonquin name. Postponing breakfast, I rigged my fly rod and set out in the canoe. Rounding the corner of the lake's southern end where the little island was located, I was treated to my first full view of Wassataquoik's narrow length. My first impression was that here was a piece of Yosemite transplanted to the woods of Maine. On its southern shore, Wassataquoik Mountain rose sharply parallel to the lake some 1,500 feet above its surface. Down one of its flanks came Green Falls, dropping the 200 feet or more the young lady at the gatehouse had promised. On the opposite shore, South Pogy Mountain rose even more steeply to a table land at an altitude of almost 3,000 feet. I drifted and paddled almost effortlessly, catching and releasing small brook trout at will. Returning to the island, I dove off the rocks at its far end—twice, in fact, out of sheer exuberance—and then stretched out in the sun to dry. At that moment, however, the blackflies returned. The early morning grace period was over.

By the time I had finished another breakfast featuring powdered eggs, the blackflies forced me into the tent. The Day-Glo orange color of its fly sheet did nothing to repel them. On the contrary it seemed to attract more; and it is no exaggeration to say that they drummed against it, making a sound like light rain for the rest of the day.

But even during the long hours of my retreat the time passed more or less agreeably. The tent seemed to have melted into the landscape of the island's wildlife, its garish color notwithstanding, and I was able to use it as a nature blind by lying on the air mattress and watching through its screened door or back window. First to catch my attention was a pair of bay-breasted warblers, a species not often seen in my home area, flitting from tree to tree near the tent. Other birds that followed included a pine grosbeak and some purple finches. At the same time there were certain birdsongs that I had not heard before.

When not so engaged, I either dozed or sat up to scratch out a few lines of my running diary. Sometimes I had eyeball-to-eyeball communion with inquisitive red squirrels that ventured very close to the tent in their search for comestibles. Even bolder was a gray jay who came within inches of the tent as it pecked at the leftovers from my breakfast. Not without reason, I now remembered, is it also commonly known as the camp jay, since it will work over campgrounds within inches of campers while they are eating. At one point between naps a lean-flanked cow moose and her calf came over to the island, but I was feeling too tired to do anything about it. Much less did I have the spine for an encounter, to be truthful, knowing that cows with young calves can be dangerous.

That night started peacefully enough, but sleep again eluded me as I began to worry about the continuing cramps in my left leg and my general ability to make the return hike the next day. There was also more screeching, as on the night before. This time I bestirred myself to investigate; it was indeed raccoons or, more specifically, two very large males engaged in a territorial fight. Their snarling and screeching seemed unbelievably loud, but eventually they either took their scrap elsewhere or stopped from sheer exhaustion. Then there was a sharp pebble or perhaps a piece of tree root that was protruding into both the flooring of the tent and my lightweight air mattress. After wriggling around in every conceivable posture within the sleeping bag trying to avoid this object, I heard the mattress puncture and slowly deflate with a mournful hissing noise. Shortly thereafter, I confess, I took another Valium, 5 mg.

The hike out the next day was breezy and lighthearted for the first three miles to Russell Pond, where I greeted the rangers cheerfully and left them some extra foodstuffs in order to lighten my pack. The seven miles from there to the road head at the Roaring Brook campground was less so, even with a somewhat lightened pack. It became in fact a rather grim march, a battle against sore feet and hunger of interest only to middle-aged desk-bound executives for whatever conclusions they may draw from it. Early in the game my stone bruise and tender left thigh forced me to favor heavily my right leg, thus effectively destroying all rhythm of walking. Then, too, my hard plastic rod case, which I now used as a poor substitute for a crutch, developed a bend, which it retains to this day. The discard of extra foodstuffs at Russell Pond proved to be a mistake; my hunger grew more intense with every mile. I had little to assuage it except a handful of Gorp and one of the repulsive meat bars.

Together these various impediments added an incredible hour and a quarter to the return journey, during all of which I did not see another living soul. Miraculously, however, familiar marks eventually began to announce the end.

At that moment my discomforts started to fade.

My last trail note reads:

> 6:30 p.m., third day. Almost hop over Roaring Brook ford. How could it have seemed so difficult? Talk, sing to myself down last pitch. Stop, regain composure and check in ever so casually with ranger. Yes very nice walk, beautiful lake, etc. It is done. *Consumatum est.* Stride gimpy-legged across parking lot, but with straight back and head up like end man in one of those Spirit of '76 tableaux, flying the flag of my faithful Yankee Doodle bag. Toss it on seat of car, then myself. Look up at sky. Cannot suppress a broad, childish grin.

I did return to Baxter State Park with my family for our Maine woods vacation later that summer. The experiment was not an unqualified success, it must be said, especially with the oldest of our six children. But the two youngest, at least, enjoyed themselves canoeing, fishing, and mountain climbing. Such was their enthusiasm for climbing, in fact, that they succeeded in cajoling their father into an assault on Mount Katahdin, choosing a route very close to Henry David Thoreau's first ascent, the last part of which he accurately described as "over huge rocks, loosely poised, a mile or more, still edging towards the clouds."

Once back home from these and other adventures, I had no clear idea of what I wanted to write. The expected inspiration did not come. Rather, my thoughts kept turning back to what I now rather too proudly considered an epic achievement in reaching Lake Wassataquoik, not to mention all the missteps and annoyances I suffered to get there, which in retrospect now seemed laughable. Perhaps this was what I should write about, I began to realize. Get it out of one's system, as the saying has it, and then the way would be clear to write something more serious.

At the time, nearly everything that had been written about camping and the outdoor life spoke of hearty meals around a cheery campfire or untroubled sleep under a starry sky. Not once did I even think of expending the energy to make a fire, relying instead on the little white-gas stove, which I came to regard as truly an Aladdin's magic lamp, a weary camper's best friend. As for sleeping under the stars, the mere thought of gambling on the absence of mosquitoes or exposing myself to the hooves of errant moose gave me the shudders. All this being so, it occurred to me to write about my experiences truthfully, to "tell it like it is" in the words of a popular expression that was just gaining currency at the time. Whatever else, it would certainly be a new approach.

In due course, therefore, I wrote an article in this vein, centered around the running diary entries like those quoted above, and sent it to a friend at the *New York Times*. After getting lost in the sports department for some months, it made its way to the Sunday "Travel and Resorts" section. Here it was accepted, which of course made me very happy. Prior to that my published writing consisted only of two short articles for the local Audubon Society bimonthly. Now, it seemed, I was off to a good start on my self-declared sabbatical.

A few weeks later I received proofs for the article, which the editor asked me to look over. Everything was in good order, I found, and I complimented him and his copy editor for a good job. But there was the matter of a title. Did he have a good one, I wondered, or did he want any suggestions?

"Oh, yes, we have a very good title," he answered and then moved quickly to tell me about possible publication dates.

On the appointed Sunday I got up earlier than usual, ate breakfast, and waited impatiently for the delivery of our Sunday *Times*. When at last it arrived, I quickly riffled through the various sections until I found "Travel and Resorts." There, spreading across the width of the third page, was my article. And there, too, was the title in what seemed to me particularly bold type. It read:

A NOVICE WOODSMAN AT 52
(WITH A LITTLE HELP FROM HIS FRIENDS)

Not only that, on the off chance readers might not understand what was meant by "his friends," a prominent sidebar in almost equally bold typeface proclaimed:

WITH AN ADEQUATE SUPPLY OF VALIUM AND CIGARETTES,
A JAUNTY BACKPACK AND A TOUCH OF MASOCHISM,
ANYONE CAN DEFEAT MIDDLE AGE AND BAXTER STATE PARK.

My instant reaction was shock, followed by a more moderate state of mild offense. Novice woodsman was the objectionable phrase. Had I not once built a splendid log cabin with only an ax and bucksaw that became the envy of all my children's neighborhood friends? Had I not successfully led a camping trip with five youngsters into the most remote and bear-infested section of the Shenandoah National Park?

My professorial older brother, who immediately called me after reading the article in the *Times,* was if anything more offended. He well remembered nights spent in the New Jersey Pine Barrens and extended trips in New Hampshire's White Mountains National Forest. Novice woodsmen we were not, he harrumphed.

But as I sat down to the initial pleasure of reading one's own words in print, I could not suppress a smile. All things considered, the article was well titled. It was my decision to confess all my foibles and missteps, even my addictions, which now in the rereading seemed more amusing than ever. Such was my original intent, in fact, as well as to forewarn innocent backpackers of my particular age group. The title reflected all those factors, I concluded.

Much encouraged, I quickly wrote a second article. The

subject this time was the Chesapeake Bay, told through a description of a waterman's workday. My friend the late Marie Rodell, with whom I sat on the board of an environmental organization and who had long encouraged me to write, thought it very good and that I should consider making it part of a book-length effort. Marie, who was a literary agent and longtime associate of Rachel Carson, then sent it to the editor of a well-known publishing house, whose advice was exactly the same. Shortly thereafter I received a contract for my first book.

"Aha!" said my older brother when I told him the news. "Success is the best revenge."

I laughed, but in truth my thoughts once again went back to the Maine woods and those who had helped me with the very first steps along the way—in getting to Lake Wassataquoik, that is to say—whose names I never knew. There was the obliging young girl at the park gatehouse, the rangers at Russell Pond, even the young man at the outdoor-equipment shop who sold me the splendid Yankee Doodle bag. I owe you my thanks, long overdue, wherever you are.

And as I do so, I feel a strong pull to return to the Maine woods and find my way to Lake Wassataquoik once more. This time it would be with proper boots and a staff, to be sure, and not during a season when people with any sense would stay out of the woods. My pack would have to be lighter, since I am now getting very close to 80 years of age. Given some preparatory workouts, though, I might just make it.

With a little help from my friends, that is.

A Short Journey to the Unknown

~

Authors who write about nature often seem to experience dramatic visions—epiphanies, we might better call them—in which the individual is revealed as a vital element in nature's grand design for planet Earth. Annie Dillard, for example, has seen a cedar tree in her backyard burning with lights, "each cell bursting with flame." Rick Bass sits on a rocky hilltop overlooking lush green fields of mint and "feel[s] my soul cutting down into the bedrock." So strong is this feeling, in fact, that he comes to believe he is one with the rock. "I, too, am becoming the earth," Bass declares. The Chickasaw writer Linda Hogan finds a large colony of flamingos wading in a Yucatán lagoon and describes the sight as "a vision so incredible and thick and numinous [that] I know it will open inside my eyes in the moment before death when a lived life draws itself out one last time before closing forever and we are drawn to these birds the way fire pulls air into it."

Those who have had similar epiphanies usually feel tempted to write about them. I have not. Quite simply, it is because I have yet to experience the state of transport that gives birth to such moments of ecstatic vision. Perhaps this will always be the case, since my moments of deepest reflection and inner calm are habitually interrupted by such commonplace thoughts as whether or not I left the dog locked outside in the backyard or paid the overdue gas bill. But I have experienced one moment, one brief and precious moment, when I came very close to transcendental vision, brought on by an uncommonly barren but dramatic landscape. It is perhaps worth the telling, especially for those readers who, like myself, await their first epiphany from the world of nature. So, too, is the journey to the place where it occurred, which, as the expression has it, was well off the beaten path.

My near epiphany took place on Ellesmere Island, the most northern and one of the largest islands in Canada's Arctic archipelago. I had gone there—it is now some 30 years past—after spending six years of foreign service assignments in the tropics, without seeing so much as a flake of snow. There thus welled up in me an irrational urge to strike out for the north. Not just anywhere in the north, that is, but to the northernmost possible lands of the Western Hemisphere, as I had already done with the southernmost.

More particularly my thoughts centered on the small town of Grise Fiord, which at 76° 24' N latitude can lay claim to being the northernmost Eskimo habitation in North America. Neighboring Greenland, it is true, has a sprinkling of Eskimo villages near Thule, some 75 miles farther north, but Greenland is not generally considered part of North America by those who ponder such matters. (Politically correct nomenclature now requires that we say Kalaallit Nunaat for Greenland and Inuit for Eskimo, but I wish to remain faithful to the usage of yesteryear, at the time of my visit.) More interesting than such considerations, however, was the promise of finding the nesting grounds of the rare ivory gull and the possibility of viewing a narwhal, the primitive whale with a long and spirally twisted tusk that is in fact a grossly elongated canine tooth. Best of all, I was told that arctic char, a spirited game fish that is in fact closely related to our North American brook trout, inhabited the lakes, rivers, and fjords of Ellesmere. As an ardent fly fisherman I became obsessed with the thought of being the first to take this handsome trout on a fly at the northern limits of its range.

The journey to Grise Fiord was a long one, even by the aviation standards of the time. By far the longest leg came first, from Montreal to Resolute on Cornwallis Island via

Frobisher Bay, aboard the now defunct Nordair, once hailed as the "workhorse of the Arctic." Getting into one's assigned seat was an adventure in itself, meaning a climb over boxes of machinery parts, a barred crate containing two growling huskies, and a small mountain of mail sacks piled up in the center aisle and on the forward seats. These discomforts aside, the flight I booked in mid-July was a good one, blessed with fine weather and the Arctic's stunning visibility that is unmatched in more temperate latitudes. I unfolded my NATIONAL GEOGRAPHIC map of Canada, spread it out on my lap, and watched it come alive from my window on the starboard side of the aircraft. Such landmarks as the peninsula on the southwest corner of Baffin Island, which bears the foreboding name of Meta Incognita, the vast Foxe Basin, the Barnes Ice Cap, the narrow and icebound Fury and Hecla Strait, and Somerset Island all passed under us, as though the landscape was being slowly unscrolled on a modern-day computer screen. Finally, there were the barren grounds and snowfields of Cornwallis Island, 600 miles north of the Arctic Circle and at the time the site of the north magnetic pole (it has since moved approximately 250 miles to the north), as well as the town of Resolute, which was then the scene of feverish prospecting for oil and precious metals.

Two days later, after a number of false starts with various bush pilots, I found passage to Grise Fiord on a twin-engine Otter with balloon tires carrying a disassembled Caterpillar tractor, tents and other camping gear, two petroleum geologists, an elderly Eskimo woman recuperating from tuberculosis, and a taciturn pilot. First stop was nearby Devon Island, where the pilot made several passes over some gravel beaches before opting for a moderately level field a mile or so inland. Here we left the Caterpillar tractor and the two geologists, who seemed visibly displeased with their new surroundings. The pilot then invited me to sit up forward in the copilot's seat, and the Eskimo lady began to cackle with pleasure when she learned that I, too, was bound for Grise Fiord, which she made very clear was her home. In this manner, we headed north and east to Ellesmere.

If the trip to Resolute had been spectacular, the shorter flight from Devon Island to Grise Fiord was unforgettable. Somewhat to my surprise I found Jones Sound, or the body of water separating Devon and Ellesmere Islands, to be icebound clear across its 70-mile expanse. Thick as it was, however, the ice was covered with a mosaic of melt pools. The water in these surface pools combined with the ice beneath them to produce an exquisite array of blue to green gradations, much like the refractions found at the waterline of floating icebergs which are so hard to describe. (Or paint, as the noted 19th-century landscape artist Frederick Church admitted after two trips to Labrador for just such a purpose.) There were also wide leads, or open passages, where the sun sparkled on blue water, in marked contrast to the dazzling white of the ice. Here the ice edges, still two to three feet thick, showed the strange inner blue that is so characteristic of high-density ice forms.

Coming closer to Ellesmere we found good numbers of plump seals at the edges of each lead, their bodies stretched out on the ice in every imaginable posture. But at first sight of the Otter, they dove quickly and gracefully back into the water, one after another, like so many Esther Williams aqua-belles in a Hollywood spectacular. My pilot companion now broke his silence to smile and say that he had seldom seen such a fine summer day or, for that matter, so many fat seals. He then went out of the way to search for more leads and to show me the hanging glaciers that sculpture the north-eastern coast of Devon Island. Shortly after getting back on course, we passed a majestic twin-spired iceberg still locked in the sea ice and probably grounded as well. I turned and twisted in my seat to keep it in view as long as possible. "That's your drinking-water supply," the pilot said, without further explanation. He then banked the plane very sharply to starboard. I turned around and saw that we were lining up for a final approach to a rough dirt-and-crushed-rock landing strip carved out of the slope of a thousand-foot mountain. After hitting the strip hard and taking one or two bounces, the Otter came to a halt. We had arrived at Grise Fiord.

As I waited for my duffle bag to emerge from the plane's tail section, a young man whose English revealed a faint trace of far distant lands welcomed me and asked me as

politely as possible what had brought me as far as Grise
Fiord. Lacking a better answer, I told him I was interested in
Arctic wildlife in general. My welcomer said I had come to
the right place and introduced himself as Bezal Jesudason.
He told me he was in charge of Grise Fiord's power genera-
tor and that I was welcome to stay in his house, which had
an extra room for visitors.

As we drove off in a battered Land Rover, Bezal
Jesudason told me he had come to the Arctic from a long
way away—from India's southern province of Madras, in
fact—and that he liked very much the challenge of living
in the far north. Very soon we were in sight of the town, the
principal feature of which was a row of about 20 small box-
shaped houses. Each of them faced south along the shore of
Jones Sound, not far from a gravel beach, where large blocks
of ice were jumbled helter-skelter by the rise and fall of the
tide. There was also a warehouse or two, a school, and a
cooperative store with a front porch that looked to be the
town's favorite gathering place. Beyond that I saw only two
larger houses, each with second stories. One of these was
Bezal's; the other, he told me, belonged to the Canadian
government's settlement manager.

That afternoon, after Bezal and I had a short walk, a
native named Akeeagok came to visit. Bezal offered him tea
and cookies, as Eskimo visiting protocols demand on such
occasions. Akeeagok ate and drank his tea in silence, punctuated only by lip smacking and grunts of satisfaction.

I broke the silence by asking about the possibilities of char fishing. Akeeagok remained silent and frowned. After what seemed like a long time he shook his head and said, no, it was not possible. The best char fishing was in a lake, still frozen, across the fjord after which Grise Fiord was named, which was also frozen. I then asked about the ivory gull nesting sites. Another silence followed, after which Akeeagok, with the help of Bezal, said that too would be impossible. No one would now want to take the long trip over the sea ice to reach them. A question about narwhals elicited what I first thought to be a more favorable response. Akeeagok at least smiled and made hand signals to imitate the narwhal's long tusk. Yes, indeed, he said, the narwhal was a very strange animal. But, no, now was not the time to see them. That would come later when larger leads and more open water permitted some boat travel.

After our guest left it began to dawn on me that Akeeagok's long silences and hesitant answers probably meant that all those limpid aquamarine melt pools on the dazzling white sea ice I had seen from the air might prove the undoing of all my plans on the ground. Could it be that the prevailing ice conditions made travel by snowmobiles too difficult or, more precisely, too wet, though the ice was certainly still strong enough?

Yes, Bezal said, it was unfortunate, but all the things I wanted to do were only possible during "ship time," as it is called in the high Arctic, when Jones Sound was largely free of ice and there was enough open water for boat travel. Sometimes this happened in July, to be sure, but August was more the rule.

That night I found it difficult to get to sleep. I worried about what I was going to do for the rest of my stay and found myself bothered by the daylight streaming all night long through the window of Bezal's extra room. Not merely light enough to see, that is, but the full light of a sun that dipped almost imperceptibly in a shallow arc above the mountainous horizon. I watched little children playing at all hours, throwing stones in a stream. A man sat smoking on the porch of the co-op. No one, it seemed, was going about any business or purposeful activity. As I would later learn, summer in the high Arctic is but one long day, when clock time and diurnal rounds are on hold and largely forgotten.

In the days that followed I took short walks along the shore of Jones Sound, visited with Eskimos in their small government-provided "matchbox" houses, and attended a square dance where my various missteps produced small gales of high-spirited laughter. I also learned that Grise Fiord was considered one of the best "hunting towns" that the Canadian government had built in recent times to resettle and house formerly nomadic Eskimos who did not want to enter the white man's wage economy. This was because Grise Fiord, previously the site of a lonely Royal Canadian Mounted Police post, had good populations of ringed and bearded seals, two species that remain in the high Arctic the year around, not to mention seabirds, fish, and a relatively high number of polar bears.

By the fifth day of my visit, however, I had a strong urge to strike out beyond town on some kind of excursion. Obviously it would have to be by land, and I thought that perhaps I could reach a large ice cap that my NATIONAL GEOGRAPHIC map showed coming close to Grise Fiord from the north. There was no telling how far it might be—5, 10, or 15 miles—judging from such a small-scale map of the Canadian Arctic. But at least it was an objective.

I set off with Bezal's good wishes and a knapsack stuffed with sandwiches, a precious orange, and a small tin of apple juice. There would be no problem with the weather, Bezal thought, since one sun-filled day had followed another all week long. This was to be expected, moreover, because the high Arctic is in fact a desert with an annual precipitation of less than three or four inches at the latitude of Grise Fiord. Much of what does occur in the form of snow tends to remain, however. Thus summer snowfields, ice caps, and glaciers.

My route at first took me along the shore, where I passed the body of a ringed seal sighted and shot amid great excitement during the square dance five days earlier. The fact that it lay there untouched gave me pause. What of the popular image of the Eskimo and other native Americans living in harmony with nature, I wondered, taking only what they need? Any further thoughts on this subject were suddenly dispelled by the demonic howling of about a dozen sled dogs—all huskies, both in name and size. As in many Eskimo communities the dogs were tethered on the outskirts of town by wire traces that ran along a stout cable. The ferocity of their growls and their teeth-baring was intimidating, to say the least. I began to run, I must confess, when it looked as though the loop of one of the wire traces might unravel. There are few Eskimo communities that have not lost a little child when this happens or, what is more common, when children venture too close as they taunt the dogs by throwing pebbles and stones.

The wolflike calls of the huskies stayed with me for a long time as I headed inland along the course of a gurgling brook that ran down a broad valley from a distant snowfield. Bezal had told me the brook supplied the town's drinking water, and I soon came upon a rubber intake hose and small electrical pump. But for most of the year the pump could not be used, when the brook was stilled by solid ice. Then came the much more difficult task—Bezal sighed when he described it—of hitching up the cargo sleds of the snowmobiles and going out to the twin-spired iceberg I had seen from the air. Once there you had to chop away at the berg, fill the cargo sleds with blocks of its thousand-year-old ice and take them home for melting. This was the "drinking-water supply" of the Otter pilot's cryptic remark. It tasted very well, Bezal had assured me.

Gradually the valley ahead grew steeper and the hiking more difficult. As far as the eye could see, the ground was covered with broken rock—a vast sea of rocks, or *Felsenmeer*, in the apposite German term used by Arctic scientists. Brown was the prevailing color of this sea, however, shading from the pale tan of cocoa powder to the light brown of natural mahogany. It seemed totally devoid of any plant life, or so I thought, at least, until I came to the nearest large snowfield. There, close to the edge of the snow, were two bright yellow arctic poppies growing between the rocks. I had first seen them on Cornwallis Island, where it is said that they along with the flowering saxifrages literally push up through the snow with the first melting temperatures. Be that as it may, the sight of the hardy little poppies lifted my spirits. I bent down to cup my hands around them and gently blew on them, as though a few seconds of my warm breath could possibly spur their growth. A useless gesture, perhaps, but understandable.

After drinking some of the snowfield meltwater, I trudged on. One hour later I reached a ridge and looked behind me. There were no more familiar landmarks. Jones Sound, the winter water-supply iceberg, the little town of Grise Fiord—all were hidden by intervening ridges or the general lay of the land. As I continued to climb, the footing became more difficult. Ahead of me was a steep talus slope with larger and sharper-edged rocks. It was no longer a *Felsenmeer*, a sea of rocks, I thought to myself; better, a

Felsensturm, or a storm of wildly jumbled rocks and small boulders, on which any misstep might mean a sprained ankle or bruised shin. As I began to have doubts about the wisdom of continuing, a jaunty little snow bunting, one of only five species of perching birds that come as far north as Ellesmere, flew by and landed on a rock not far ahead of me. It was clearly a male, dressed in his peak mating plumage of black and white. He bobbed up and down on the rock, looking at me and chirping in what seemed a very inquisitive manner. It seemed almost as though he were asking me what I was doing so high up in the barren domain that was his private mating ground. He then flew to the top of the next ridge, where he began to sing melodiously. I decided to follow.

"A smooth, swelling skyline of pure white, high up against a clear blue sky, is often a land traveler's first view of an Arctic ice cap: it is a quintessentially Arctic sight." So reads an Arctic guidebook in my library. The description is exactly what I saw from the top of the next ridge—the blinding white of a huge, shallow-domed mass of ice set against a blue sky, dotted only with a few puffy-white fair-weather clouds.

At last I had reached it, or so I thought, since it did not look to be far away. How interesting it would be to examine close at hand! Would the ice cap be advancing or spreading outward along its periphery, spawning what are known as outflow glaciers? (An ice cap is essentially a mass of ice lying on relatively level ground; the weight of accumulating snow and ice on its underlying layers will force the cap to expand outward in tongue-shaped lobes, which may become moving glaciers when they reach downhill terrain.) Or would it be retreating, sending out torrents of meltwater from its scalloped tongues? I continued my climb in double time.

A half-hour later I had climbed the talus slope, but the ice cap seemed as distant as ever. Ahead of me was a narrow snowfield leading up a more gentle incline. The easy footing it provided was a merciful relief, but the farther up I walked on the granular snow, the more I became uneasy. Below me a faint rushing and rumbling sound came from deep down under the snow, a sound I had once heard before on the summit cone of New Hampshire's Mount Washington on a hike in June. Undoubtedly it was a subsurface meltwater stream, but I could not see an outlet anywhere along the edge of the snowfield. Perhaps the water was backing up behind an ice dam or a ridge in the permafrost ground. No doubt it would eventually break out from under the snow, somewhere down the slope. I therefore walked more carefully, stepping gingerly, one foot after another.

The end of the snowfield brought me up to a U-shaped saddle between two mountains that might well have been formed by a hanging glacier in geologic time. The ice cap was no longer visible, hidden somewhere above and behind me by the steepest slope of the saddle. This slope was so steep, in fact, that I knew instinctively it was beyond my ability. I therefore sat down, tired and discouraged, convinced I had picked a bad route. Any close encounter with an ice cap might have to wait another day.

Presently, after catching my breath and examining the contents of my lunch bag, I looked out from my perch at the edge of the saddle. Spread out before me was a great valley, a vast basin six or seven miles in its longest dimension, surrounded by low mountain ranges. It seemed a land to itself, completely hidden and cut off from the surrounding terrain. Only the monochrome light tans and browns of its rock fields were the same, interrupted here and there by snow patches and small ice caps on some of the surrounding mountains. What struck me first was the silence, a vast and enveloping silence that was almost palpable, broken only by small whispers of wind. I therefore closed my eyes and "listened to the quiet," as a yoga instructor had once instructed me. Almost immediately a sense of calm and well-being came over me.

When I opened my eyes again the thought came to me that perhaps I was the first human being to view the valley, or at least to have set foot on the exact spot where I had found such excellent vantage. Spread out before me was what seemed to be a sterile land, not yet touched by any plant or animal succession. There were no bright yellow poppies or blue saxifrage pushing up through the rocks or snow. There were no birds, no songs of snow buntings or larkspurs, nor gulls or other seabirds flying overhead. There were not even any mosses or lichen to be found on the rocks near where I sat. Why, therefore, would any arctic foxes or other animals climb up to this barren land, much less the Eskimos who hunt them?

Yes, it was entirely possible! I could be the first to see this land, this unknown valley. I half-closed my eyes in meditation and felt such a strong sensation of lightness and power that I thought I might actually levitate. At the same time some uncommonly wild and preternatural images raced through my mind. Very clearly it came to me that I was witnessing the land at the dawn of creation. Snatches of half-forgotten biblical phrases came quickly to mind. *On the third day . . . Let the waters divide . . . dry land . . . God called it earth . . . saw that it was good. . . .* And here was this dry land called earth laid out before me for my sole and private contemplation! In the sheer exuberance of the moment I decided to take possession of the valley in the manner of a Spanish conquistador. Cupping my hands around my mouth, I shouted at the top of my voice, "I CLAIM THIS LAND IN THE NAME OF GOD AND THEIR SOVEREIGN MAJESTIES—"

Suddenly a frightening noise came from above me. It sounded as though freight trains were rattling down the U-shaped valley behind me, passing close by. Rather than levitate, I now felt myself sinking down and trying to hide behind a large boulder. When I dared to peer out from my perch, I saw what looked like a small tornado picking up rocks as large as grapefruits and whirling them in the air. Within seconds a smaller one—call it a good-size dust devil—followed in its wake. Their noise and aftermath echoes seemed to continue for a long time as the two twisters danced way down into the valley, their trails marked by spirals of rock dust. At the same time a cold draft of air blew down from above. What in the world was happening, I wondered, on such an otherwise calm and clear day?

There was no time to think. Now my senses were assailed by the sound of rushing water, and I looked down to see a slight depression in the snowfield somewhat like the first signs of a crevasse running downhill from the center of the field. Sure enough, a stream of gushing water now surged from the lower end of the field. What was worse, the water seemed to be following my exact route of ascent, gaining volume all the while.

The signs were all too clear. I had defiled this untouched land with such a foolish and vainglorious act. More, I had broken the second commandment. Now the heavens were speaking. Quickly I munched half a sandwich, stuffed the other half in the pocket of my parka, and started my descent, humbled and contrite.

Of the trip down, I prefer to say very little. What stands out in my mind is that I had to cross the newborn melt stream not once but three or four times. As a consequence, since I had gone over the top of my felt-lined Sorel boots, my feet were numb from the ice water. When I walked fast or almost ran downhill trying to warm them, I risked several tumbles. It was necessary to slow down and use caution, I realized, cold feet or no.

By the time I approached the coast, I was more than glad to be greeted by the snarling huskies and, not too much later, arrive at Bezal's in time for tea. I remember how happy I felt in dry socks and warm slippers, laughing and wolfing down the tea cookies. Akeeagok was there to offer me a guttural welcome, and he and Bezal both laughed when I tried to tell them the events of the day, punctuated by my best efforts at sign language. Soon the chairman of Grise Fiord's Recreation Committee, an Eskimo named Pijamini, dropped by with a friend to announce another square dance in the recreation hall that night. He and his friend seemed greatly amused as I tried to excuse myself by an elaborate pantomime of climbing a high mountain and then descending, footsore and weary, with an aching back.

After a splendid supper with Bezal, who had been such a good friend, I looked out my bedroom window. The sun was only beginning the slow parabola of its descent and the air was still so clear that when I looked out over the sea ice, still dotted with the exquisite blue-green melt pools,

I fancied I could see clear across the Jones Sound to the loom of the land on Devon Island. Later that night I stopped packing for the flight out the next day to look out the window a number of times. Little children were staying up all hours, throwing pebbles in the stream or playing hopscotch. Older men were sitting on the co-op porch, smoking as before. Presently people from different parts of town started converging on the recreation hall like iron filings to a magnet. It was not really night, I had to remind myself, but just another moment in the one long day that is the high Arctic summer.

I remember going to sleep gratefully, thinking God was in his heaven and all was right with the small world of Grise Fiord. It had been a good trip, after all, no matter the absence of ivory gulls, fishing, or the chance to see narwhals.

In the long years since, I have learned two truths. The first is that the strange little twisters that scared me away from the hidden valley may have been by-products of what meteorologists call katabatic or "downhill" winds from the Greek *katabasis,* meaning "descent." These occur when cold air, always heavier than warm, sinks close to inclined ground and picks up speed as it goes down. If the cold air passes over ice caps or glaciers, it quickly becomes still colder and therefore heavier until it bowls down the mountain at extreme speeds. If the katabatic winds meet warmer air rising uphill (as would certainly have been the case from the sun beating down on the light brown rock fields of the hidden valley), the two opposing air masses clash and shear. They are then apt to produce vorticity, in the language of meteorology, meaning anything from the little eddies of dust devils to the spinning vortexes of death-dealing tornadoes.

The other and more important truth is that it is unwise to claim or even think of the land God called Earth as one's private or exclusive domain. I have therefore never done so again. Nor do I any longer await the kind of transcendental event or ecstatic vision other writers have experienced. That sparkling day in the hidden valley, close by an Ellesmere ice cap, was event enough for me. And, best of all, the vision of it remains bold, clear, and as starkly beautiful as ever.

SADDLEBACK

~

On the southeast coast of the island of Vinalhaven, Maine, there is a small promontory called Arey's Neck. In order to sail from the Neck out into the broad reaches of Penobscot Bay, Maine's largest, it is necessary to pick your way through a labyrinth of shoals, small islands, half-tide rocks, and ledges bearing such names as Sister, Mitten, Clam, Green, House, and Halibut. An early edition of the venerable *Cruising Guide to the New England Coast* told yachtsmen who had doubts about approaching this part of Vinalhaven simply to pass it by. More recently the guide warns:

> The waters to the southwest, south, and southeast [of Vinalhaven] are extremely dangerous. The tide runs swiftly between rugged and unmarked ledges and the whole area is wide open to the sweep of the North Atlantic. If one gets ashore [aground] in this area, he might well lose his boat.

Sound advice, to be sure, but hardly comforting to those whose home anchorage is in these waters. Such at least was the case not many summers ago when my wife and I first visited one of my sons-in-law and his family in a farmhouse on Arey's Neck.

On the first evening of our visit, I walked from the house through meadows and heather thick with bayberry, wild rose, and lupine down to the rocky shore of the Neck. In the near waters were most of the celebrated ledges, each marked by small white curls of breaking waves. Farther out the seas crashed heavily on Halibut Ledge, marked by a red nun buoy.

I sat down by the shore and kept looking seaward for a long time. A filmy haze was drifting in from the sea, casting both land and water in a strangely beautiful half-light. It was the kind of light sometimes seen on the Maine coast that leaves the viewer wondering whether a dense fog may roll in or the sun's slanting rays will set clear and bright below the horizon. At the moment, however, I did not much care what happened, or which might come first. It was enough to be there, taking it all in.

As it turned out the hazy fog won the contest, obscuring the view of the opposite shore of Isle au Haut, the "high island" so christened by Samuel de Champlain. But just before the fog closed in, I saw a strange object halfway across the water. At first glance it appeared to be the back of a sea monster. Or was it a surfaced submarine with the "sail" of its conning tower setting out to sea? But after focusing my binoculars, it became a rocky ledge on top of which was a small and stubby building roughly the shape of an inverted cone. Could such an odd structure possibly be a lighthouse? In a matter of minutes there was no doubt. A bright light flashed on and off very quickly. After a few seconds it flashed again. Yes, it was a lighthouse, the strangest I had ever seen.

Back in the farmhouse I consulted the appropriate nautical chart and quickly found the light. Saddleback Ledge, the chart said, "Fl 6s 54ft HORN," meaning that the lighthouse flashed white every six seconds at a height of 54 feet above mean high water and that it was equipped with a foghorn. Further inspection showed that it stood almost in the middle of the mouth of East Penobscot Bay, three miles from the seaward tip of Isle au Haut and three and a half miles from the southeast corner of Vinalhaven Island. Indeed, it seemed wide open to the sweep of the North Atlantic, as the *Cruising Guide* had promised. But, happily to say, I also discovered that Saddleback provided a good mark to steer for from the tip of Arey's Neck through all "the rugged and unmarked ledges" out to the red nun at Halibut Ledge. Thereafter, it was clear sailing.

As the summer wore on, it became my habit to walk down to the shore almost every evening to bid good night to the light on Saddleback Ledge. Sometimes it would be after dark, when the lighthouse gave its quick white flashes every six seconds against a brilliant night sky crowded with bright stars. At other times it would be twilight, when the automated light's reassuring flashes first became apparent. In the daytime, too, I often went down to the shore with my grandchildren, who were happy to collect periwinkles or look for little green crabs stranded in tidal pools while I watched Saddleback in its various moods. In heavy weather great plumes of spray shot up from the seaward side of the ledge. And once, when a passing hurricane left enormous surges in its wake, one great swell seemed to envelop all of the ledge and the tower.

All these observations confirmed my first impression. Saddleback Ledge was indeed the strangest, the oddest light I had ever seen. Further study revealed other and more significant superlatives. The conical tower was certainly short, the shortest of any on Maine's outer islands, in fact, standing only 42 feet above its rocky base. It may also be the strongest of all Maine's lighthouse towers, having been built of curved and interlocking blocks of granite two-and-a-half-feet thick. Or so, at least, we are led to believe by one I. W. P. Lewis, a crusty inspector who in 1842 called Saddleback "the only establishment on the coast of Maine that possesses any claim to superiority over its fellows . . . and the only one ever erected in New England by an architect and an engineer."

These technicalities aside, Saddleback was invariably described as "one of the most lonely outposts on the Maine coast," "the most inhospitable," and "extremely hazardous for landing." Perhaps Charles McLane and Carol Evarts, the indefatigable authors of the four-volume *Islands of the Mid-Maine Coast,* have summed it up best:

> The Saddleback Ledge station was surely one of the most hazardous and lonely on the Atlantic coast. The island is barely large enough to hold the tower and equipment necessary to keep the light operating; there is no soil of any type on the ledge. In the great storms, when the island was awash, the keeper and his family were obliged to retreat to the tower.

All of these descriptions, all of these superlatives only heightened my interest in Saddleback. I soon found that not only did keepers and their families retreat from their station house to the tower at times of great storms, but for the earliest years at Saddleback there was probably no dwelling place other than the tower itself. It is hard to imagine how a family could possibly live year in and year out in the tower's cramped upper quarters. But at least in one case a child was born there. In September 1843, or four years after the light was built, we are told that the wife of Keeper Watson Hopkins gave birth to a baby girl. A week later a boat crew arrived to take Mrs. Hopkins and her child to the mainland. In so doing, however, the crew dropped the baby into the sea for a brief moment in the always difficult task of getting underway. But the child evidently suffered no ill effects from this icy dunking. Vinalhaven's leading historian, Sidney L. Winslow, tells us that the baby, christened

Margaret, grew up to marry a Civil War veteran named William Kittredge "and came to be one of our town's well-known and best beloved citizens."

Sometime around the turn of the century a proper and commodious two-story house was built in the lee of the tower for the keeper and crew. By then, too, Saddleback had been designated a "stag station," for men only, served by a head keeper and two assistants. Even so the men were occasionally forced to retreat to the tower, since its base on the highest part of the island was only 12 feet above sea level at high tide and therefore sometimes awash in heavy weather. Indeed, the house was always in danger of being swept away during severe storms. After the great March storm of 1947, Keeper Alamander Alley reported that the house was "almost completely washed away in a matter of a few hours," and that the fog bell that had served for over a hundred years was "now silent in the ocean grave, never to ring again." It all but broke Alley's heart, he confessed "after working hard for twenty-two years . . . trying each day to keep this place in good order."

When it was not being battered by the sea the light was occasionally bombarded by migrating birds, which often seem to have a fatal attraction to lighthouses at night during gale and storm conditions. In February 1927 Keeper W. W. Wells and his assistants were surprised when what he called "a cannonading . . . of ducks and geese" began to batter the house and in some cases break through its windows.

Finally, Wells tells us:

> Just when I thought the cannonading had ceased one
> big sea drake struck the plate glass in the tower lantern,
> and came through without asking for a transfer. When
> he struck he broke up the works. Before he stopped he
> put out the light and broke prisms out of the lens. The
> bird weighed over ten pounds.

Wells's "sea ducks and drakes" were most probably surf or white-winged scoters, which habitually fly single-file, low to the water in long and irregular lines. Other keepers have reported Canada geese striking their lights and thereby providing the stations with tastier fare than the fishy "coots," as scoters are called in New England. And tragically, the tiny warblers and other small land birds that are blown off their migratory courses by severe storms.

But even after the dwelling house had been rebuilt, repaired, and buttressed with a heavy-timber protective wall, Saddleback Ledge remained a lonely and undesirable post. Records of the Coast Guard and its predecessor United States Lifesaving Service show that a number of keepers and assistants could not stand life on the Ledge and were replaced after one or two months. Others seem to have been challenged by Saddleback's hardships and stuck it out for 10 to 20 years.

Even so, loneliness and the ceaseless tedium of carrying coal and lamp oil up to the tower, trimming the wicks, watching for flareups, polishing brass, and otherwise keeping the station in good order remained a constant problem. When the *Maine Coast Fisherman* published its first edition in 1946 with a section for letters from lighthouse keepers entitled "Life at the Light Stations," Saddleback soon provided the most frequent and more lengthy contributions. In May 1947 the redoubtable Alamander Alley reported with some excitement that a woodcock had landed on the island and flown right into the boathouse. But he was still waiting for boats with the supplies and tools necessary to repair the shambles left by the great storm of the previous March. He had "searched every gulch and crevice on the old place" for tools to undertake repairs himself "but never found as much as a monkey wrench."

Much as keepers disliked the heavy weather, they delighted in boasting about which station suffered the worst. "When a whale up in Nova Scotia gives a big splash, three days later it is so rough here that lobsters crawl back into deep water," the keeper of Mount Desert Rock wrote. When Captain "Bug" Osgood, the popular keeper at Saddleback from 1948 to 1951, was transferred to the Curtis Island station near Camden Harbor well inside Penobscot Bay, he wrote: "I came here June 11th from Saddleback, and what a change! It gets rougher in the wash dish out there than it does around here. My wife has to throw water on the windows so I can sleep."

Bad weather and winter's ice storms aside, life at the Saddleback station was so uneventful and visitors so rare that bulletins to the *Maine Coast Fisherman* sometimes took on a plaintive note or relied more and more on minutiae. After a remarkably mild winter in 1949, substitute Keeper Edward Giffin told of a very heavy snowfall in March and allowed as how at least "it was something to look at besides the water and rocks." Others went on at length to chronicle the latest mischief of their cats and dogs. When Keeper Alley first announced his retirement, he was genuinely worried about the disposition of his pet cat and hoped "she may stay out here and live the rest of her days if the boys don't object to her after I leave." Sometimes, too, the station hands must have felt an irresistible urge to get outdoors and take a good walk. When assistant Jerry Lawrence tried to do this, he stumbled in a cleft in the rocks and sprained his wrist. "I told him to be more careful and keep on the lawn and sidewalks more," Alley wrote.

Summer, then, with its hope of good weather and the promise of more visitors was always welcomed by the station crews. Then it was that as many as a hundred sail, both fishing smacks and cargo schooners, could be counted on a clear day at the Ledge. Visitors were still rare, even though landings presumably became easier after 1885 with the installation of a "landing derrick," which swung a boom and tackle out over the water, at the end of which was a bosun's chair. Nevertheless it was often difficult to catch the boom end from a heaving dory. "It might look easy to the fellows on the station," Keeper William Wells warned, "but to the man in the boat nothing looks certain." We know, however, that hardy yachtsmen occasionally attempted it. Photographs at the Vinalhaven Historical Society show tweed-coated men awaiting their turn aboard a small schooner while one of their lady friends swings ashore in the chair, fully attired in a flowing turn-of-the-century dress and a broad-brimmed hat with a veil. "We had a good lobster lunch and everyone enjoyed having them call," a station hand reported of one such visit. "We hope they come again."

Then, too, there was always the potential for good fishing from March onward. Now a thing of the past, inshore spawning runs of cod, haddock, and halibut came almost as regularly as clockwork in Penobscot Bay. Ted Ames of Stonington remembers how good the fishing was when his grandfather Andrew Bennett was keeper at Saddleback from 1914 to 1925. "Back then nobody had the technology to wipe the fish out," Ames says. "We really had a fisherman's paradise here. You could hand-line all the big halibut anyone ever wanted."

In time, as I learned more and more about Saddleback, it no longer seemed enough simply to gaze at it from Arey's Neck. I would have to go to it. I would have to land on that "extremely hazardous" and "most inhospitable" island. At first I dreamed of living there at different times of the year to watch the changing face of the sea and to gain some small

idea of what life on the Ledge must have been for the keepers. But such an idea was highly impractical on a number of
counts, not the least of which was the requisite permission
from the Coast Guard. I therefore gladly accepted when my
friends Frank and Delphine Eberhart volunteered to take me
to Saddleback aboard the *Hound,* their sturdy 60-foot sloop,
which they had skippered to Greenland, Russia, and many
other distant destinations. Not only that, the Eberharts
owned a Maine peapod, or the handsomely designed dou-
ble-enders that were the small boat of choice for most of
Maine's difficult lighthouse stations.

Accordingly, we set sail from Vinalhaven on a quiet day in
late August with the jaunty little peapod firmly in tow. The
sea was calm, with only the lightest of airs, as the *Hound* rose
and fell to gentle swells that caressed her bow. By the time
Saddleback was less than a mile distant, however, the swells
were no longer so gentle. Indeed, a quick look through
binoculars showed the frothy white of breaking waves along
many parts of the island. Then, as we stood in to shore, I
found somewhat to my dismay that the tide was low. This
meant that great festoons of seaweed—the always slippery
rockweed and bladder wrack, to be exact—hung from every
rock along the shoreline. Nevertheless Frank and Delphine
boarded the peapod and urged me to follow suit, while my
wife Kathleen and Frank's mate stood off on the *Hound.*

We first approached a gully where the station's boat slip
had once been, only to find that some small seas were

occasionally breaking noisily over a promontory that usually provided the slipway with a modicum of shelter. With Frank at the oars we proceeded to the northernmost tip of the island, where after some reconnoitering we found a small rock at the water's edge that appeared to be mercifully flat, weed covered though it might be. As we drew near to it, we were met by a guard force of gray seals lolling in the surf. Much larger and less common than Maine's ubiquitous harbor seal, they challenged our presence with a vigorous display of splashy dives and tail slapping. Frank, however, paid no heed to their intimidations and darted in and out between the bigger swells—a task for which the double-ended peapods are ideally suited—to deposit first Delphine and then me on the flat rock. Fortunately Delphine, who is young, strong, and athletic, was able to offer me a helping hand as we slithered and crawled up the glistening slopes of seaweed until at last we set foot on dry rock. I had landed on Saddleback Ledge.

Our first moments on the island proved a pleasant surprise. The rhythmic clash of wave and rock, so ominous when we first approached, now became music to our ears; and the sea air mixed with the pungent smell of drying seaweed was both agreeable and invigorating. Seagulls greeted us with their usual clamor, while tiny shorebirds stopped pecking in weed-filled cracks in the rock and flew around us peeping in alarm. A yellow flash signaled the presence of a migrating warbler, which immediately flew off to resume its southerly course. The noisy gray seals, perhaps aware that we wished them no harm, stopped their splashing and kept a respectful distance. Saddleback Ledge, the most lonely and inhospitable island, seemed to be coming alive.

But the lighthouse itself, the top of which was barely visible above the upward slope of the rocks ahead, remained our primary objective. We therefore set off in high spirits, only to find the island everywhere riddled by deep fissures and crevices. It was sometimes necessary to retrace our steps, in fact, when some of them proved too wide to jump. And instead of the pungent sea air, there was the stench of decay wherever some of the crevices had collected storm water, now stagnant and in some cases holding the broken bodies of small gulls or terns.

As we stepped carefully along I could not help but think of Alamander Alley searching "every gulch and crevice" for tools to repair the station house or warning his assistants "to keep on the lawns and sidewalks." Soon enough, however, we reached the island's summit, now probably all of 22 feet above the water at full ebb tide. And there, of course, was the Saddleback Ledge lighthouse, looking strong, solid, and as superior as Inspector I. W. P. Lewis had claimed over a century and a half earlier. The interlocking blocks of granite, so well cemented, looked as though they would last for centuries to come. Most of the tower's windows looked to be exactly the same as those shown in 19th-century photographs. So, too, with the cupola holding Saddleback's powerful light, along with its walkabout and protective balustrade. The only new element was a small automatic foghorn bolted to the walkabout platform. Every few seconds it let forth with a high-pitched and piteous cry that seemed a poor match for the dull roar of the heaving surges that now crashed on the rocks that formed the seaward ramparts of Saddleback Ledge.

Everything else in the tower's immediate vicinity, however, was a picture of abandonment and neglect. Only the rubble of the brick foundations of the station house remained, plus some markings where the house had nestled against the leeward side of the tower. A comfortable two-and-a-half-story building, painted Coast Guard red and white, it was one of a number that had been blown up after automation in the 1950s by a Green Beret amphibious assault team in a program to destroy a few offshore lighthouses that has long since been halted by the state of Maine.

Not far away were two iron rails lying at odd angles at the top of the gully where the boat slip descended to the water's edge. Presumably they were all that is left of the railway and carriage where the station's peapod once sat poised, ready for rescues, visitors, or the arrival of inspectors or supplies. Not far from the rails were the iron reinforcement rods that held up a heavy timber protective wall on the southeast side of the tower. All the rods were weirdly twisted and bent, witness to the power of wind and wave and the prevailing direction of winter storms. Near the base of the slipway the steel pole of the landing derrick still stood upright, rusted and minus its boom and bosun's chair.

As we prepared to leave, I was surprised by the sight of two monarch butterflies, first spotted by Delphine, which did much to lift my spirits. We took pains not to disturb them as they clung to the rocks, characteristically opening and closing their wings. They would need all their strength, we imagined, to make their next landfall. Then, to my greater surprise I found two clusters of tiny white flowers with yellow centers—probably asters of one variety or another—tenuously rooted in a crack in the rocks. Again, Saddleback Ledge, the most lonely and inhospitable island, seemed to be coming alive.

Back aboard the *Hound* we sailed away on a freshening breeze toward Isle au Haut. From a distance the lighthouse tower itself looked to be alive, or at least an organic part of the island, an outgrowth, as it were, of the rocks on which it stands and just as timeless as they. I kept looking back at it for a long time, even with binoculars, until called to action as the *Hound* came about from one course to another.

It has often been said that everyone loves a lighthouse. "Their physical presence speaks of absolute service to mankind," as Philip Conkling, director of Maine's Island Institute, has well expressed it. "Their lights, beaming across a dark wilderness of sea, are widely recognized as beacons of care, integrity, and perseverance." To which we need only add they are among the handsomest of monuments along our coasts, witness the thousands of camera-carrying tourists that visit the more accessible stations every summer.

This being so, I cannot easily explain my love affair with Saddleback, which is neither handsome nor much photographed even by passing yachtsmen. Perhaps it is enough to say that I will always look forward to returning to Arey's Neck and looking out over the labyrinth of shoals, small islands, and half-tide rocks, out beyond the red nun at Halibut Ledge, to the stubby little lighthouse on Saddleback Ledge. And knowing that it will always be there, for many years to come.

Author's Note

~

ooks can have unexpected beginnings. For some time I have been eager to share some of the more exotic journeys—the odysseys of the title—and the more interesting observations of nature that I have had the good fortune to make, and it would please me to say that the idea for this collection sprang from deep in the wellspring of my creative instincts. But such was not the case. Rather, this book began with a request that seemed an intrusion on precious time I had reserved for other purposes.

The request came from my friend David Williamson of the Nature Conservancy. The Conservancy was then putting together an anthology of nature writing, Williamson explained, based on the theme of its "Last Great Places" campaign. Several authors had already agreed to write pro bono contributions. He wondered if I would be willing to do the same, especially if it were an essay on the Chesapeake Bay.

At the time, however, I was trying to finish an ambitious work of history for an academic press. It had already taken me far too long, or so many years that I am still embarrassed to confess their number. The path ahead, quite obviously, was to finish this work once and for all without interruptions. But when David told me my contribution need not necessarily be about the Chesapeake Bay, concerning which I had already written much, but rather on any other natural area of my choosing, his request became slightly more attractive. Then, even as I doggedly forged ahead as slowly as ever with my history, constantly checking and rechecking archival references or rearranging footnotes, the thought came to me that perhaps a break might be salutary. I would take a busman's holiday to write about a subject I loved.

In the words of a timeworn advertising slogan, the result was a pause that refreshed. The reader may find one of the fruits of this pause, in fact, in the form of the first essay in this collection, revised to serve as a prologue to those that follow. Not only that, the pause gave fresh impetus to my academic labors, which were soon finished with dispatch. My thanks, therefore, to David Williamson and the Nature Conservancy editors.

These things done, my time was at last my own, luxuriously free of major commitments. But I soon found that what some call the comforts of retirement quickly palled. The remedy, of course, was to continue with more of what I liked best to write. Encouraging me along the way were Jay Tolson and Robert Wilson, editors of the Woodrow Wilson International Center for Scholars *Wilson Quarterly* and the National Trust for Historic Preservation's bimonthly *Preservation,* respectively, who published some of my subsequent work. My thanks to them as well, therefore, and a hearty recommendation to readers to sample the broader horizons both have brought to their publications.

A writer friend of mine has said that some of his best stories often have a way of taking on a life of their own. I know well what he means and have taken steps to forestall this tendency, which manifests itself most often in the retelling of experiences that took place many years ago. In this regard I am deeply indebted to a number of persons who have helped to jog my memory or fill in gaps caused by the loss of field notes or diaries. Alexander Boyd has helped me round out the tragically short life of his older brother, John, my companion in dinosaur excavations in east-central Utah and the first of my college classmates to die in action in World War II. For expert advice on the dinosaurs John and I helped to uncover, I owe much to James H. Madsen, Jr., of Dinolab, Holladay, Utah, who is the reigning expert on *Allosaurus,* the carnivorous dinosaur found in extraordinary number in the quarry where we worked. Jim has also been invaluable in bringing me up to date on the fast-changing world of dinosaur paleontology, and it has been my pleasure to offer him details of the early Princeton University excavation season in 1941, which he has incorporated in his exemplary history of the quarry site, now known officially as the Cleveland-Lloyd Dinosaur Quarry and a designated Department of the Interior United States Natural Landmark. At Princeton Peggy Cross has kept me informed of the fate of the University's Geology Museum and the de-emphasis of paleontology, sad to say, within what is now known as the Department of Geology and Geophysical Sciences.

Similarly, Terry Jesudason of Resolute Bay, Northwest Territories, Canada, has helped me recall the general setting of the little Arctic hamlet of Grise Fiord, now Ausuittaq, the scene of my visit with her late husband, Bezal. Terry continues Bezal's work at High Arctic International, which is an ideal base for polar expeditions and tourist travel in the high north latitudes.

There has been one exception, one slight aberration in this quest for accuracy. In the title essay Henry Buck is a fiction; he is rather an amalgam of two of my school classmates, neither of whom want their true names known. But my memory of what happened upon crawling "Into the Porcupine Cave" and the subsequent consequences has been helped by other classmates and my older brother, Charles, who ventured into the cave two years before me.

Similarly, I cannot much remember the wording of the stern reprimand the school's rector gave Henry and me for our forbidden escapade, no doubt because we were both quite nervous about what dire punishment he was about to mete out. The rector, too, is therefore an amalgam, in this case of the many stern New England schoolmasters of an older generation whose oratorical excesses I have often suffered.

I once remember reading a passage I had written on the mating practices of the Atlantic blue crab to the Smithsonian Institution's resident carcinologist, as experts in crabs and other crustacea were once called. My description of the crabs' mating was highly naturalistic—anthropomorphic is now the preferred term—so it was with some apprehension that I asked him what he thought of it. "There is nothing wrong or incorrect in what you have written," he answered. "But I certainly wouldn't express it that way."

That brief dialogue has remained a cautionary tale for me ever since. True, anthropomorphic writing by scientists is today more common, now that we have come to realize that many animals experience some of the same emotions as we do. Still, I continue to submit my scientific exegeses to the same test—first, in the name of accuracy and, second, as a restraint against naturalistic excesses, to which I confess I am sometimes prone.

Among those who have helped me to provide a measure of apposite scientific background, I would like to single out Uldis Roze of Queens College, City University of New York. Dr. Roze's work has taught me much about the North American porcupine, surely one of the least known and most misunderstood of the familiar animals of our forests and woodland lots. His book *The North American Porcupine* in the Smithsonian Institution's Nature Books series is a model of its kind and a pleasure to read.

Many persons have helped me to find my way amid all the recent interest in *Orcinus orca,* or the dolphin also known as the killer whale. Among them I particularly remember Jim Mastro of Antarctic Support Associates, an intrepid scuba diver in Antarctica's frigid shelf waters, who in the course of an e-mail exchange from McMurdo Sound once wrote to me:

> I have held a camera underwater not five feet from an orca, with several others nearby. They seemed as curious about me as I was about them, but never threatening. This was a large pod of about 100 animals. I would never do that if the pod was small.

Mastro's underwater discoveries along the Ross Ice Shelf heightened my existing interest in the differences between the two communities of orcas—large resident pods of fish-eating orcas, that is to say, and very small transient pods of "killers," living almost entirely on the flesh of other warm-blooded animals—which inhabit both our Pacific

Northwest and Antarctica. This interest eventually led me to A. Rus Hoelzel, of the National Institutes of Health, who has found that the two are indeed genetically distinct. By the same token Claudio Campagna, director of Argentina's *Fundacíon Patagonia Natural,* and Rodolfo Werner, one of his able field scientists, have given me first-hand accounts of the seasonal visits of killer whales to snatch sea lion cubs off the beaches of Patagonia's Valdés Peninsula, not to mention how the parent whales train their young to do the same.

Others who have contributed their knowledge in the rapidly expanding field of orca studies include Howard Garrett of the Center for Whale Research at Friday Harbor, Washington; Douglas Hand, author and artist; Sue Pressman, consultant to the American Society for the Prevention of Cruelty to Animals; and Claire Fleming of the American Museum of Natural History. Jim Antrim, vice president and general curator of SeaWorld California, and Murray Newman, former director of the Vancouver Aquarium, have provided valuable insights into the research value of aquarium studies and the improved health and birth records of orcas in captivity.

A visible and very audible member of the animal kingdom of the tropical rain forest of the Americas is the howler monkey. This being so, it is surprising that it has not received nearly as much scientific attention as, for example, the baboons and other primates of the Old World. One who has given the howler due study is Katherine Milton of the

University of California, who has carried out field studies of the Central American howler monkeys for some 25 years at the Smithsonian Institution's Barro Colorado Island in the Panama Canal Zone. Her good counsel and her published work on howler foraging strategies and troop interactions have been most enlightening.

Very little of the fascinating history of Saddleback Ledge, surely one of Maine's most hazardous lighthouse stations, would be known to me without the assistance of Roy Heisler and Esther Bissell, who direct the Vinalhaven Historical Society, a model of its kind, on Maine's Vinalhaven Island. The same is also true of Dave Getchell of Appleton, Maine, who served as an editor of the *Maine Coast Fisherman*. Dave alone had the good sense to keep bound volumes of this publication, now the *National Fisherman*, which include a treasury of letters from the brave and stoic keepers of the Saddleback Ledge Lighthouse. My thanks to him, therefore, and also to Harry Duvall of Needham, Massachusetts, and Ken Black, director of the Shore Village Museum in Rockland, Maine, both former "wickies" of the Coast Guard's lighthouse service, for instructing me in some of the more technical aspects of their profession.

I have benefited from the advice of many friends. As always, my brother, Charles K. Warner, has played a prominent role in this regard, as have most of my six children, who remain my most faithful reader-critics. My former Smithsonian colleague David Chalinor; author Phyllis Theroux; and college and school classmates J. Otis Carney and Paul G. Pennoyer, Jr., all belong as well in this category.

Finally, I would like to thank Kevin Mulroy and Kevin Craig of the National Geographic Book Division for their good advices. And for their patience, let me quickly add, with a writer who is totally ignorant of the new world of computer scanning and paperless transmissions.